ᵃDAYBOOK
ꜰₒᵣ Nurse Leaders
ₐₙₐ Mentors

Sigma Theta Tau International
Honor Society of Nursing®

SIGMA THETA TAU INTERNATIONAL

Editor-in-Chief: Jeff Burnham
Acquisitions Editor: Fay L. Bower, DNSc, FAAN
Editorial Team: Jeff Burnham, Carla Hall, Melody Jones, Jim Mattson, Jane Palmer, Linda Puffer

Cover Design by: Rebecca Harmon
Interior Design and Page Composition by: Rebecca Harmon
Cover photo: Copyright Alan Briskin

Printed in the United States of America
Printing and Binding by Printing Partners

Sigma Theta Tau International
550 West North Street
Indianapolis, IN 46202

Visit our Web site at www.nursingknowledge.org/STTI/books for more information on our books.

ISBN-10: 1-930538-50-2
ISBN-13: 978-1-930538-50-4

06 07 08 09 10 / 5 4 3 2 1

Table of Contents

Introduction VII

January 1

February 15

March 28

April 42

May 55

June 69

July 83

August 97

September 111

October 124

November 138

December 152

Bibliography 173

Index of Authors....................................... 175

Introduction

We live in a rapidly changing world, particularly within health care. Flexibility and adaptability are demanded in order to keep up and move forward. As members of the helping professions, nurses are on the front line of patient care and transformational health care. As nurse leaders and mentors, you lay down powerful stepping stones on the path leading to actualization of an inner vision or professional dream. You carry the torch for those following behind, and light the way into the future.

Perhaps you were once mentored, and now find you are in a role to offer guidance to others. Leadership is learned, and while state-of-the-art organizational management techniques can be taught, and we can emulate great leaders or teachers, it is the growth of the inner self that truly shapes us into leaders. Professional relationships that encourage self-reflection, self-awareness, and honesty create the foundation of an authentic leader. Integrity and trust are essential cornerstones of mentored relationships, enhanced by shared knowledge and mutual respect for each other.

Each of us is part of a cycle of learning and growth, as inevitable as the seasons you will travel through a year. This daybook reminds you to pause, day to day, and accept the gifts of each day. This book offers words of inspiration collected from many wise mentors and leaders, so take a moment to enter a thoughtful space that will nurture you throughout your journey. For the times when you need the *right* words to summarize what you have learned, or affirm what you *know,* that is when you may find just the right quote.

Meaningful actions are pivotal to good leadership. Personal and professional growth, productivity, a sense of shared purpose, and the achievement of the goals we set for ourselves and our relationships require close attention and commitment. We are all part of a never-ending cycle of life and learning, expressed through our work and our passions. Take care of your inner self even as you attend to the needs of the outer world and others. Within this small book, find the inspiration and encouragement every day to be a nurse leader for tomorrow.

Fay L. Bower, DNSc, FAAN

January

JANUARY 1

Leadership is legacy—it is ensuring that the enterprise goes beyond and is composed of more than the individual. Leadership is making a difference and causing a difference to be made.

—Marla Salmon, RN, ScD, FAAN
Pivotal Moments in Nursing, Volume II

JANUARY 2

We can't accept the status quo in healthcare. We can't afford to only share our research, our leadership, our expertise among ourselves. If we believe we can't make a difference on a broader plane, we won't.

—Mary Wakefield, RN, PhD
Reflections on Nursing Leadership

JANUARY 3

Instilling a desire in nurses to take a leadership role in the future of this profession is a challenge some days. For the willing participant, however, embracing leadership is rejuvenating.

—Beth Houser, RN, DNSc, FNP-C, CNAA, and Kathy Player, RN, EdD
Reflections on Nursing Leadership

JANUARY 4

I have always surrounded myself with the best people to do their jobs, because I do not want to learn what they already know better than I do.

—Shirley Sears Chater, RN, PhD, FAAN
Pivotal Moments in Nursing, Volume I

JANUARY 5

My philosophy has always been to turn negatives into positives. Barriers increase my determination—motivate me. When barriers are placed in my path, they are almost like an affirmation that others see potential in me that I do not see.

—Eloisa G. Tamez, RN, PhD, FAAN
Reflections on Nursing Leadership

JANUARY 6

Positive leadership styles are those in which leaders develop, stimulate, and inspire followers to exceed their own self-interests to achieve a higher purpose.

—Maria R. Shirey, RN, MS, MBA, FACHE, CNAA, BC
Reflections on Nursing Leadership

JANUARY 7

Learn how to act instead of react to the changing world by associating yourself with those who are succeeding. Learn about tomorrow's work world so that you can be in the right place when critical decisions are made.

—International Leadership Institute
Honor Society of Nursing, Sigma Theta Tau International
Reflections on Nursing Leadership

JANUARY 8

Kind words can be short and easy to speak, but their echoes are truly endless.

—Mother Theresa

JANUARY 9

Being a team player involves more than just following the leader, it requires you to be proactive when the occasion calls for it.

—Eleanor Sullivan, RN, PhD, FAAN
The Rules of the Game

JANUARY 10

When you take the elevator to the top floor, send it down for somebody else.

—Richard Carmona, RN, MD, MPH, FACS
Pivotal Moments in Nursing, Volume II

JANUARY 11

If we are serious about career development—personally and organizationally—
we need to take the time to look within. This means "crossing the street" into
the darker, unlit areas and examining the connection between our daily work
tasks and our sense of life purpose. It means exploring our values and finding
or strengthening relationships that provide us with the support and guidance
needed to turn our inner realizations into tangible action.

—Eric Klein, BA
Reflections on Nursing Leadership

JANUARY 12

I have had many more problems based upon my gender than my color. I could
have ended my career, just with a little incident, and sat down and said, "Oh
well, I can't go any further than here," but I didn't choose to do that. As a
matter of fact, I chose to use it as an incentive for me to get moving.

—Clara Adams-Ender, RN, MSN, CNAA, FAAN
Reflections on Nursing Leadership

JANUARY 13

Mentors do not have to be in charge. In fact, the best mentor is often not the boss or someone in a high-level position.

—Fay L. Bower, DNSc, FAAN
Building and Managing a Career in Nursing

JANUARY 14

Change is inevitable, though often frightening. Together we can face into the spiral of change with faith that the apparent chaos will yield to self-organization and new growth.

—Diane L. Stuenkel, RN, PsyD
The HeART of Nursing, Second Edition

JANUARY 15

Nurses are teachers wherever they practice. From academic institutions to the halls of hospitals and homes, nurses educate. They impart theory, principles, research, and techniques to another generation of nurses, to healthcare colleagues, to policymakers and patients, families and communities.

—Nancy Dickenson-Hazard, RN, MSN, FAAN
Reflections on Nursing Leadership

JANUARY 16

> [I] learned that preparing tomorrow's leaders to surpass one's own accomplishments is the mark of a professional.
>
> —Linda Aiken, RN, PhD, FAAN, FRCN
> *Pivotal Moments in Nursing, Volume I*

JANUARY 17

> The professional decision maker is self-aware, courageous, sensitive, energetic, and creative.
>
> —Bessie L. Marquis, RN, CNAA, MSN, and Carol J. Huston, RN, CNAA, MSN, DPA
> *Leadership Roles and Management Functions in Nursing, Fourth Edition*

JANUARY 18

> Whether addressing issues of access, delivery, or discovery, we can accomplish far more collectively than we can as single entities. ... Ron Heifetz, a contemporary author on leadership, calls it "getting up on the balcony and looking down on the dance floor to keep the big picture in view." One of the most difficult tasks of collaboration, the "big picture" approach requires repeatedly asking, "Will this help us achieve our goal?" Continual focus on the mutually agreed outcome is the most likely path to success, for without it the partnership is doomed.
>
> —Nancy Dickenson-Hazard, RN, MSN, FAAN
> *Reflections on Nursing Leadership*

JANUARY 19

[It is] not about my leadership, it is how much I can develop *your* leadership that is important.

—Joyce Clifford, RN, PhD, FAAN
Pivotal Moments in Nursing, Volume I

JANUARY 20

If a leader stays on message, then others will hear the message.

—Angela Barron McBride, RN, PhD, FAAN
Reflecting on 30 Years of Nursing Leadership: 1975-2005

JANUARY 21

When you experience success, share it by mentoring new nurses and those who will benefit from your unique skills wherever they are on their career path.

—International Leadership Institute
Honor Society of Nursing, Sigma Theta Tau International
Reflections on Nursing Leadership

JANUARY 22

Seek state and national leadership opportunities that will train and refine your voice, giving it new clarity and volume. Never be satisfied with the legacy you have already created because opportunities abound for those who want to make a difference.

—Beth Houser, RN, DNSc, FNP-C, CNAA, and Kathy Player, RN, EdD
Reflections on Nursing Leadership

JANUARY 23

Nurses bring knowledge, skills, and awareness to the policy table as well as to the patient's side. It is only through the facilitation of debate and discussion that we will resolve the issues we face in healthcare and society at large.

—Iain Graham, RN, Med, MSc, PhD
Reflections on Nursing Leadership

JANUARY 24

Use of research evidence to guide clinical and operational decisions is a necessity in healthcare delivery. Chief nurse executives (CNEs) and their leadership staff set the stage and culture for evidence-based practice (EBP). ... Providing this leadership is not for the faint of heart.

—Marita G. Titler, RN, PhD, FAAN, Laura Cullen, RN, MA, and
Gail Ardery, RN, PhD
Reflections on Nursing Leadership

JANUARY 25

As I have matured professionally, I have come to appreciate the lasting stamina of mentoring relationships in directing professional lives. I have also come to believe that mentoring is a professional responsibility, as well as an opportunity for growth. For the profession to flourish, all of us are obligated to be both mentors and protégés through our career span.

—Patricia E. Thompson, RN, EdD
Reflections on Nursing Leadership

JANUARY 26

You have to be able to lead yourself before you can lead others.

—Nancy Dickenson-Hazard, RN, MSN, FAAN
Reflections on Nursing Leadership

JANUARY 27

Leaders must create structures where renewal is infused within the work culture.

—Karlene M. Kerfoot, RN, PhD, CAAN, FAAN, and Steven S. Ivy, MDiv, PhD
Reflections on Nursing Leadership

JANUARY 28

Mentors are key to the advancement and sustainability of evidence-based practice (EBP) in institutions. ... Research indicates that nurses who are mentored by colleagues with expertise in EBP come to believe in EBP, gain confidence in it and, as a result, help promote its implementation.

—Bernadette Mazurek Melnyk, PhD, CPNP, NPP, FAAN, and Ellen Fineout-Overholt, RN, PhD
Reflections on Nursing Leadership

JANUARY 29

Practicing nursing taught me communication skills, scientific skills, management, writing, speaking, and business skills. Few professions afford this much diversity and opportunity.

—Nancy Dickenson-Hazard, RN, MSN, FAAN
Reflections on Nursing Leadership

JANUARY 30

Through educational programs, publications, and technology experts, learn what tomorrow's technology will be able to do. This way you will help to lead the way in making technology an asset to your career.

—International Leadership Institute
Honor Society of Nursing, Sigma Theta Tau International
Reflections on Nursing Leadership

The art of nursing involves having the ability to sense the meaning of a situation and the authenticity to share self and metaphysical experience.

—Cynthia Bostick, RN, CS, PhD
The HeART of Nursing, Second Edition

February

FEBRUARY 1

You don't want to oppose the vision of others. ... You should utilize the group
vision to obtain motivation through collaboration.

—Ada Sue Hinshaw, RN, PhD, FAAN
Pivotal Moments in Nursing, Volume I

FEBRUARY 2

We will only effectively address health issues by changing infrastructure and
systems. Nursing as a team member with other stakeholders from within
society can help achieve this. Only by working as a team will we do the work of
drawing together many perspectives to find solutions.

—Iain Graham, RN, MED, MSc, PhD
Reflections on Nursing Leadership

FEBRUARY 3

Become active in professional, political, and community organizations, first as
a volunteer and eventually as a leader. Your new skills will serve you best if the
right people know about you when someone with your talents is needed.

—International Leadership Institute
Honor Society of Nursing, Sigma Theta Tau International
Reflections on Nursing Leadership

FEBRUARY 4

The best lessons I learned came from the school of life.

—Grayce Sills, RN, PhD
Pivotal Moments in Nursing, Volume II

FEBRUARY 5

I was but a fledgling nurse.
My nursing knowledge was limited, and not well versed.
Your standards were HIGH
Your expectations were GREAT
You inspired me to see, nursing was my fate.
Education and wisdom, you provided.
Mentoring and coaching it never subsided.
As I reflect upon my achievements,
it becomes evident to me,
that, because of YOU,
I am a better ME!

—Sharon A. Brown, RN, MSN
The HeART of Nursing, Second Edition

FEBRUARY 6

When expectant parents have their first sonogram, they are often surprised at the image on the screen. But when the health professional tells them, "There is your baby," that blur takes on a powerful meaning. ... In the early stages of growth, many projects are little more than a blur. It takes a trained eye to interpret the indistinct, fuzzy image as evidence of real progress. Mentors spot the signs of growth before they are obvious to the untrained eye. They name the emerging reality and honor the natural process of birth and growth.

—Eric Klein, BA, and Nancy Dickenson-Hazard, RN, MSN, FAAN
Reflections on Nursing Leadership

FEBRUARY 7

To produce the leaders of tomorrow, we need to see the best of our profession move seamlessly across teaching, research, and clinical activity.

—Tony Butterworth, CBE, PhD, RMN, RGN, FRCN, FmedSci, FRCPsych
Reflections on Nursing Leadership

FEBRUARY 8

Authentic leaders understand their own purpose and search for meaning along life's journey.

—Maria A. Shirey, RN, MS, MBA, FACHE, CNAA, BC
Reflections on Nursing Leadership

FEBRUARY 9

On Richard Carmona: With each leadership step he took, Rich remembered his roots and took his nursing experience of collaboration, communication, and compassion with him.

—Beth Houser, RN, DNSc, FNP-C, CNAA, and Kathy Player, RN, EdD
Pivotal Moments in Nursing, Volume II

FEBRUARY 10

This is the way many are socialized into the nursing profession: Stay objective; don't get too close to the patient; don't share yourself; be professional. ... Some nurses are willing to enter the world of suffering, and they lead the way. ... They have heard the cries of pain and acknowledged the person beyond the pain.

—Judy Sadler, RN, PhD
Reflections on Nursing Leadership

FEBRUARY 11

Loretta Ford is known to frequently end speeches with a quote from Aristotle that she feels should be uppermost in our minds: "Where your talents and the world's needs cross, there lies your vocation."

—Beth Houser, RN, DNSc, FNP-C, CNAA, and Kathy Player, RN, EdD
Pivotal Moments in Nursing, Volume I

FEBRUARY 12

Develop your spoken and written communication skills so you can speak and write about what you know and value. Hone your skills in a second or third language, then use them to communicate with colleagues and consumers from other countries.

—International Leadership Institute
Honor Society of Nursing, Sigma Theta Tau International
Reflections on Nursing Leadership

FEBRUARY 13

Inclusive leadership is the act of bringing together individuals from diverse backgrounds to accomplish a shared vision. This is no small feat since the full realization of this goal requires the participation of all four generations currently shaping the nursing profession: the veterans, the boomers, the Xers and the Nexters, and each generation brings with it individual values, expectations, skills and work styles (Zemke et al., 2000).

—Jennifer L. Hobbs, RN, BSN
Reflections on Nursing Leadership

FEBRUARY 14

Vernice was acutely aware of the value of empowering "the staff nurses down in the trenches," so as professionals they would feel they had the authority to properly do their job.

—Beth Houser, RN, DNSc, FNP-C, CNAA, and Kathy Player, RN, EdD
Pivotal Moments in Nursing, Volume I

FEBRUARY 15

The World Health Organization (WHO) has identified nurses as essential healthcare professionals and major assets to the world's population. WHO has recognized, therefore, that if nurses are utilized to their full potential, there is an increased capacity to improve health outcomes for the global community we serve.

—Genevieve Gray, RN, MSc, Dip Adv Nurs Studs, Dip Ned, CM, FRCNA, FCN (NSW)
Reflections on Nursing Leadership

FEBRUARY 16

Futurists give attention and energy to aligning inner and outer forces around them. Futuristic individuals are mindful of time and its influence. They recognize the importance of timing and use this understanding to direct the course of events.

—Nancy Dickenson-Hazard, RN, MSN, FAAN
Reflections on Nursing Leadership

FEBRUARY 17

Nursing is a profession in need of change and mentoring is our link to the future.

—Melodie Daniels, RN
Reflections on Nursing Leadership

FEBRUARY 18

Build an area of expertise and others will seek you out.

—Gretta Styles, RN, EdD, FAAN
Pivotal Moments in Nursing, Volume I

FEBRUARY 19

Reflecting on my own experiences and hearing the stories of colleagues have convinced me ... that effective mentors are what make the difference between leaving nursing or staying and building a satisfying career. What would have happened if I had not had mentors? Most likely, I too would have left nursing.

—Pamela R. Cangelosi, RNC, PhD
Reflections on Nursing Leadership

FEBRUARY 20

We each, by bringing our unique energies to share, enrich all within our circle upon the earth. As such, we are much more than the sum of our individual selves, and our co-creations are much more than any one could be capable of alone.

—Linda Jerzack, RN, NP
The HeART of Nursing, Second Edition

FEBRUARY 21

One's image of what one does in the nursing profession may not fit with what is going on in the industry at a particular time. The real question a leader must ask is, "How are you planning to correct your professional course when the environment no longer matches your original vision?"

—Florence Schorske Wald, RN, MN, MS, FAAN
Pivotal Moments in Nursing, Volume II

FEBRUARY 22

There are certain times when you simply can't compromise. When you believe in something and are convinced it is the right thing to do, acting on principle makes for some difficult days, but it sure helps you sleep better at night.

—Melanie C. Dreher, RN, PhD, FAAN
Reflections on Nursing Leadership

FEBRUARY 23

Learn practical financial principles from the very beginning. ... By becoming financially savvy, you can achieve security in your personal and professional life.

—International Leadership Institute
Honor Society of Nursing, Sigma Theta Tau International
Reflections on Nursing Leadership

FEBRUARY 24

Do not wait for leaders; do it alone, person to person.

—Mother Theresa

FEBRUARY 25

I think true leaders think about what it means to be a leader; they don't just take it for granted. Leading is a privilege that is earned.

—Richard Carmona, RN, MD, MPH, FACS
Pivotal Moments in Nursing, Volume II

FEBRUARY 26

Nurses individually and collectively need to package our information, not in the language of research journals, but in the parlance of policymakers. These efforts don't require establishing a vehicle for giving campaign contributions or employing lobbyists to carry an agenda. They do require nurses to engage with their elected officials at state and federal levels and to do what nurses often do best—educate.

—Mary Wakefield, RN, PhD
Reflections on Nursing Leadership

FEBRUARY 27

The mentor's mind is like a mirror—impartially reflecting back the truth of the person and the situation. Through this precise and nonjudgmental mirroring, the mentor invites others to engage truthfully in their life, to accept and express their greatness.

—Eric Klein, BA, and Nancy Dickenson-Hazard, RN, MSN, FAAN
Reflections on Nursing Leadership

FEBRUARY 28

Finding fault is criticism, while critique is challenging, expanding or changing the viewpoint to improve the outcome. Criticism can be demoralizing, while critique is elevating and necessary for professional growth. Nurses need to learn how to offer and embrace the gift of critique.

—Leah Curtin, RN, DSc, MS, MA, FAAN
Pivotal Moments in Nursing, Volume II

Notes

March

MARCH 1

I never thought of being anywhere other than the top.

—Vernice Ferguson, RN, MA, FAAN, FRCN
Pivotal Moments in Nursing, Volume I

MARCH 2

I call it the positive way of looking at obstacles—not to look at them as something to stop you, but rather something you may, indeed, decide to go under, over, around, or through.

—Clara Adams-Ender, RN, MSN, CNAA, FAAN
Reflections on Nursing Leadership

MARCH 3

Leaders must be very clear about their own beliefs before they are able to lead others. To be an effective leader, mentor and influential role model, one must clarify his or her values and goals and be aware of their influences on future leaders.

—Billye Brown, RN, EdD, FAAN
Reflections on Nursing Leadership

MARCH 4

Linda [Aiken] also feels strongly that nurse leaders have a responsibility to mentor, develop, and convince future leaders that they can do things that they hadn't considered possible. According to Linda, Claire Fagin is the best example of this in nursing leadership. She muses that "after spending five seconds with Claire, you are convinced you can do something you never dreamed that you could do." Under this kind of leadership, anything is possible, and barriers become unexpected opportunities for creative solutions.

—Beth Houser, RN, DNSc, FNP-C, CNAA, and Kathy Player, RN, EdD
Pivotal Moments in Nursing, Volume I

MARCH 5

By knowing the hopes, aspirations, and dreams of those they lead, leaders are able to forge unity of purpose by breathing life into their constituents' needs and showing them how they can realize their hopes through a common vision. In doing so, leaders create passion for the compelling group dream.

—Nancy Dickenson-Hazard, RN, MSN, FAAN
Reflections on Nursing Leadership

MARCH 6

To accomplish leadership goals for our profession, we must rid ourselves of the anti-intellectualism that abounds throughout our discipline and our educational programs. It is time to reach upward in our programs to prepare nurses at the highest clinical level.

—Joyce Fitzpatrick, RN, MBA, PhD, FAAN
Reflections on Nursing Leadership

MARCH 7

Personal networks are composed of like-minded friends whose eyes light up when they see you. They are the people who make you feel good or recharged. They love you and want to make you happy. Making time for your personal network is absolutely essential for motivation.

—Fay L. Bower, DNSc, FAAN
Building and Managing a Career in Nursing

MARCH 8

Every Friday afternoon Joyce [Clifford] would meet with four or five nurse leaders for "popcorn time" to discuss what they had accomplished that week at the unit and organizational levels to improve the nurse-patient relationship and patient care quality.

—Beth Houser, RN, DNSc, FNP-C, CNAA, and Kathy Player, RN, EdD
Pivotal Moments in Nursing, Volume I

MARCH 9

The leader lives in the space between action and potential, anticipating the next step and translating the process for others.

—Tim Porter-O'Grady, RN, PhD, FAAN, and Kathy Malloch, RN, MBA, PhD, FAAN
Quantum Leadership

31

MARCH 10

I have an almost complete disregard of precedent, and a faith in the possibility
of something better. It irritates me to be told how things have always been
done. I defy the tyranny of precedent. I go for anything new that might
improve the past.

—Clara Barton

MARCH 11

Nurse education is also a key component of developing emerging nurse leaders,
leaders who aim to transform their own practice and inspire others to do the
same. Such leaders require the skills of reflective practice to enable other
practitioners to identify contradictions between desired practice and actual
practice.

—Dawn Freshwater, RGN, PhD, BA, RNT, FRCN
Reflections on Nursing Leadership

MARCH 12

Many times nurses don't feel they are in a position to make changes, but I want
them to understand that nurses can make change happen providing they have
both persistence and visibility for their work.

—Claire Fagin, RN, PhD, FAAN
Pivotal Moments in Nursing, Volume I

MARCH 13

Being at the table meant bringing valued data and leadership to the discussion, and Loretta [Ford] often led the charge. She helped to motivate, organize, and maintain the focus of the nurse practitioner movement through some very difficult leadership moments.

—Beth Houser, RN, DNSc, FNP-C, CNAA, and Kathy Player, RN, EdD
Pivotal Moments in Nursing, Volume I

MARCH 14

As is the case in health systems in most countries, nurses make up the largest professional workforce in Australia and deliver the majority of direct patient care. Increasingly, the practices of nurses are seen to have a direct impact on patient outcomes, particularly in the areas of satisfaction with care, successful early discharge, infection control, and a wide range of other desirable health outcomes.

—Alan Pearson, RN, ONC, DipNEd, DANS, MSc, PhD, FCN(NSW), FINA, FRCNA, FAAG, FRCN
Reflections on Nursing Leadership

MARCH 15

Recognize the talent of others and acknowledge it.

—Gloria Smith, RN, PhD, FAAN
Conversations With Leaders

MARCH 16

Authentic leaders possess five distinguishing characteristics: purpose, values, heart, relationships, and self-discipline.

—Maria R. Shirey, RN, MS, MBA, FACHE, CNAA, BC
Reflections on Nursing Leadership

MARCH 17

Leaders who challenge the status quo and put themselves on the line by telling people what they need to hear and do, rather than what they want to hear and do, risk resentment. But good things seldom happen without searching for opportunities and changing to take advantage of them.

—Nancy Dickenson-Hazard, RN, MSN, FAAN
Reflections on Nursing Leadership

MARCH 18

Health futures work must be both imaginative and plausible, but it also has to confront the will to act. To be helpful, it has to influence learning, encourage commitment to action, and inspire those involved to question their sacred assumptions.

—Eleanor Sullivan, RN, PhD, FAAN
Creating Nursing's Future

MARCH 19

While at UCSF, Rheba [de Tornyay] discovered a lifelong mentor in Helen Nahm. In later years when faced with a significant challenge, Rheba would often find herself asking, "What would Helen do?" Helen Nahm's leadership advice had been explicit, practical, and logical—*think of the consequences.* She taught Rheba to think not only of the consequences of a decision but the consequences of not making a decision.

—Beth Houser, RN, DNSc, FNP-C, CNAA, and Kathy Player, RN, EdD
Pivotal Moments in Nursing, Volume I

MARCH 20

The one thing that a leader has to do is appreciate that everybody is partly right.

—Daniel J. Pesut, APRN, BC, PhD, FAAN
Contemporary Issues in Nursing, Volume II

MARCH 21

Too much emphasis is placed on accelerated nursing programs as a way to meet demand [for more nurses]. The emphasis should be on mentoring, not fast tracking. Fast tracking will produce technicians, not effective nursing leaders.

—Theresa A. Granger, MN, ARNP, NP-C
Reflections on Nursing Leadership

MARCH 22

You know, I am not very interested in the past because that is gone, but I am very interested in tomorrow. ... Ask me about tomorrow.

—Margaret McClure, RN, PhD, FAAN
Pivotal Moments in Nursing, Volume II

MARCH 23

Developing strong mentor connections is a shared responsibility and partnership among nurses—and potential nurses—at all levels of the profession. Building mentor relationships is a transformational act that will foster both individual and collective power in our professional work.

—Connie Vance, RN, EdD, FAAN
Reflections on Nursing Leadership

MARCH 24

For in the end, each master guides and enlightens the neophyte.
Each teacher and mentor must
Pursue the truth,
Perfect the praxis, and thus,
Preserve the discipline.
As the work of change is not that of the elusive muse;
The discipline speaks to the world only through the dance of each practitioner, the
Individual nurse.

—Carla A. Bouska Lee, PhD, ARNP, C, CNS
The HeART of Nursing, Second Edition

MARCH 25

In revealing self, leaders risk criticism, rejection, and, for some political leaders, even physical harm. On the other hand, leaders who are not exceptionally clear in word and action about what they believe, and who fail to communicate what is most significant, may lose credibility and respect. Achieving effective leadership lies in one's capacity to model the way, thus earning respect and the right to lead.

—Nancy Dickenson-Hazard, RN, MSN, FAAN
Reflections on Nursing Leadership

MARCH 26

I am not just a researcher, educator, administrator, or practitioner; I am interested in developing all aspects of nursing to achieve true professional status, with all of the rights, responsibilities, and recognition attached to other well-established professions.

—Gretta Styles, RN, EdD, FAAN
Pivotal Moments in Nursing, Volume I

MARCH 27

The real test is what the leader does when the opportunity presents itself. Opportunities are often lost without hard work. On the other hand, an opportunity seized and developed with a good outcome creates numerous future opportunities.

—Rheba de Tornyay, RN, EdD, FAAN
Pivotal Moments in Nursing, Volume I

MARCH 28

Now the challenge for healthcare and for the workplace is that it be fluid,
flexible, focused, portable, and mobile.

—Tim Porter-O'Grady, RN, PhD, FAAN
Contemporary Issues in Nursing, Volume II

MARCH 29

Vernice [Ferguson] expresses the importance of the phrases "never take a back
seat" and "never take no for an answer" as key motivators in her life. She never
believed nurses should take the back seat to physicians or take anything less
than what is offered to physicians. "What is good enough for the doctor is good
enough for me and the nursing staff."

—Beth Houser, RN, DNSc, FNP-C, CNAA, and Kathy Player, RN, EdD
Pivotal Moments in Nursing, Volume I

MARCH 30

According to Kouzes and Posner (2002), leadership is a dynamic process
that results in extraordinary accomplishments when leaders engage in five
common practices: 1) model the way, 2) inspire a shared vision, 3) challenge
the process, 4) enable others to act, and 5) encourage the heart. These practices
are available to anyone, in any situation, in any organization—once he or she
accepts the mantle of leadership.

—Nancy Dickenson-Hazard, RN, MSN, FAAN
Reflections on Nursing Leadership

MARCH 31

In responding to the opportunities and demands of the information age, nurses can both influence and be influenced by the growth and dissemination of knowledge. In the process, new nurse leaders will come to the forefront. Who will they be? Perhaps one of them will be you.

—F. Sevgi Hatýpoðlu, RN, PhD
Reflections on Nursing Leadership

Notes

April

APRIL 1

I think the best thing we can do for our profession is to believe in ourselves and in each other. Whatever career path a nurse chooses, to me, it should be for the right reason—coming from a place of passion. You do it because it's something you really believe in and not because you're tired of working weekends or holidays, or you're burned out.

—Vickie L. Milazzo, RN, MSN, JD
Reflections on Nursing Leadership

APRIL 2

The right title allows you to join the circle, but it is not the true influence.

—Florence Schorske Wald, RN, MN, MS, FAAN
Pivotal Moments in Nursing, Volume II

APRIL 3

Leaders are pioneers and early adopters of innovation. They understand that change, risk, experimentation and failure are all part of the landscape.

—Nancy Dickenson-Hazard, RN, MSN, FAAN
Reflections on Nursing Leadership

APRIL 4

In addition to mentoring others, nurses need to find themselves a mentor. The professional growth that occurs in these relationships is priceless. All of us must take the initiative for furthering our development.

—Patricia E. Thompson, RN, EdD
Reflections on Nursing Leadership

APRIL 5

Those of us who are nurses need to be more proactive about who we are and what we do. If we aren't, who will be?

—Hila J. Spear, RN, PhD
Reflections on Nursing Leadership

APRIL 6

Increasingly, Singapore's nursing leaders are recognizing that in a competitive, fast-moving and uncertain world, they have to depend more and more on individuals, particularly the young nurses, who have the potential to contribute new ideas and innovations and who have the courage to push for changes before opportunities disappear.

—Roselin Ang, RN, MSN, and Long Chooi Fong, RN, MSc
Reflections on Nursing Leadership

APRIL 7

Every organization needs both perchers and nesters. The nesters have the painstaking task of establishing order and building a system, while the perchers, like me, come along and enrich it and fix it, and often leaving their debris behind.

—Grayce Sills, RN, PhD
Pivotal Moments in Nursing, Volume II

APRIL 8

Nurses are what make or break the health systems and the health status of people. Every day a multitude of nurses leads a multitude of patients to well-being.

—Nancy Dickenson-Hazard, RN, MSN, FAAN
Reflections on Nursing Leadership

APRIL 9

Today's leaders must find ways to engage, challenge, nurture, and retain future nurse leaders.

—K. Lynn Wieck, RN, PhD, Margaret Prydun, RN, PhD, and Terri Walsh, RN, MS
Journal of Nursing Scholarship

APRIL 10

We assume most men and women choose to become nurses because they want to help people live well. Our hope is that they will see the unlimited possibilities of nursing to change the world.

—Melanie C. Dreher, RN, PhD, FAAN, Dolores J. Shapiro, RN, PhD, and Micheline Asselin, RN, MPA, MSN, CHPN
Healthy Places, Healthy People

APRIL 11

Leaders are responsible for future leadership, for identifying likely leaders, and for developing and nurturing those potential leaders. Having a mentor is important for potential leaders, but so is having a role model. Not every individual will be able to select and contract with an official mentor, but we all have had role models at some time during our career.

—Billye Brown, RN, EdD, FAAN
Reflections on Nursing Leadership

APRIL 12

Everything a nurse executive does requires explicit and refined communication skills, and underlying that is the ability to build good relationships.

—Margaret McClure, RN, EdD, FAAN
Pivotal Moments in Nursing, Volume II

APRIL 13

Mentoring requires a high degree of involvement, commitment, and energy. It demands an acceptance, an amicability, respect, trust, and confidence in self and others. It necessitates a willingness to be challenged, take risks, and work with uncertainty.

—Eric Klein, BA, and Nancy Dickenson-Hazard, RN, MSN, FAAN
Reflections on Nursing Leadership

APRIL 14

I enjoy being backed into a corner in situations where I have to fight my way out.

—Gretta Styles, RN, EdD, FAAN
Pivotal Moments in Nursing, Volume I

APRIL 15

Pathways to leadership are diverse. For many, it is important to seek higher levels of education, such as the BSN, MSN, and PhD. For some, it is important to take advantage of classes and seminars at work or become certified in a specialty area. Finally, for others, it is important to reach way beyond their workplace and even their local institutions of higher education and apply for one of the numerous leadership [development] opportunities that are available nationwide.

—Susan B. Hassmiller, RN, PhD, FAAN
Reflections on Nursing Leadership

APRIL 16

When leaders enable others with trust and confidence, people take on risks, make changes, and keep the vision alive. In this way, leaders also turn members of their team into leaders.

—Nancy Dickenson-Hazard, RN, MSN, FAAN
Reflections on Nursing Leadership

APRIL 17

Authentic leaders lead with heart and compassion. They care for themselves and the people they lead.

—Maria R. Shirey, RN, MS, MBA, FACHE, CNAA, BC
Reflections on Nursing Leadership

APRIL 18

Will you be a hero in your daily work? We may give you an institution to learn in, but it is you who must furnish the heroic feelings of doing your duty, doing your best, without which no institution is safe.

—Florence Nightingale

APRIL 19

You can think of balancing your life in two ways: One I call both/and, while the other is either/or. A lot of people think they can *either* go the professional route *or* choose to be a wife and mother. I like the both/and approach...You can have *both and* do both. You can enjoy a family life while leading a professional life. I really believe I am one of those people who had it all. While it was not always easy, the support services I established and the friendship of my colleagues made it possible.

—Shirley Sears Chater, RN, PhD, FAAN
Pivotal Moments in Nursing, Volume I

APRIL 20

Individually, positive leadership results in staff and patient satisfaction. Organizationally, the outcome is competitive advantage.

—Maria R. Shirey, RN, MS, MBA, FACHE, CNAA, BC
Reflections on Nursing Leadership

APRIL 21

He [Richard Carmona] asked the leaders to make a decision if serving the underserved and indigent population was the hospital's mission.

—Beth Houser, RN, DNSc, FNP-C, CNAA, and Kathy Player, RN, EdD
Pivotal Moments in Nursing, Volume II

APRIL 22

Resiliency is the process of identifying or developing resources and strengths to flexibly manage crisis to gain a sense of confidence, mastery, and self-esteem, and to achieve a positive outcome.

—Janice Post-White, RN, PhD, FAAN
Reflections on Nursing Leadership

APRIL 23

Leadership judgment is called judgment because certainty is missing.

—Tim Porter-O'Grady, RN, PhD, FAAN, and Kathy Malloch, RN, MBA, PhD, FAAN
Quantum Leadership

APRIL 24

In this fast-paced demanding environment, nurse leaders must cultivate the financial and political skills to be innovative.

—Bessie L. Marquis, RN, CNAA, MSN, and Carol J. Huston, RN, CNAA, MSN, DPA
Leadership Roles and Management Functions in Nursing, Fourth Edition

APRIL 25

[A good boss is] the person who will be challenging, have high expectations, and be a good collaborator.

—Marla Salmon, RN, ScD, FAAN
Pivotal Moments in Nursing, Volume II

APRIL 26

Unlike the formal teaching experience, the teaching that occurs during a mentor relationship is usually spontaneous, individualized, and time constrained.

—Fay Bower, DNSc, FAAN
Building and Managing a Career in Nursing

APRIL 27

You owe it to yourself—and to your patients—to hone your skills to a higher level. You can play a role in creating the safest and best care around. To do so, however, you must keep increasing your knowledge level, expanding your decision-making capabilities and improving your skills in all areas, including clinical and administrative.

—Susan B. Hassmiller, RN, PhD, FAAN
Reflections on Nursing Leadership

APRIL 28

Lessons learned through the rich experience of others are the most valuable educational tools for illustrating both what works and what doesn't work. To experience the full appreciation of successful risk taking in leadership, one must acknowledge that the same amount of energy and passion can bring setbacks or failures in pursuit of a goal. It is the fear of failure that prompts some to choose to disembark on their journey, while the other leader will hunker down and come back stronger.

—Beth Houser, RN, DNSc, FNP-C, CNAA, and Kathy Player, RN, EdD
Pivotal Moments in Nursing, Volume I

APRIL 29

Whether it may or may not look politically correct, one has to stand by what they believe to be the right thing.

—Grayce Sills, RN, PhD
Pivotal Moments in Nursing, Volume II

APRIL 30

Leaders live their lives backward. They envision what things will look like, believe in the dream, and have the confidence and desire to make it happen. The picture of the future is the force that invents action and movement.

—Nancy Dickenson-Hazard, RN, MSN, FAAN
Reflections on Nursing Leadership

May

MAY 1

I have failed more times in my life than I have succeeded. The difference is
I just continued to get up. Ultimately, I just got up one more time than the
person who failed.

—Richard Carmona, RN, MD, MPH, FACS
Pivotal Moments in Nursing, Volume II

MAY 2

Current leadership approaches tend toward the three-stage process of
individual transformation, namely, self-directed learning, critical reflection,
and transformative learning.

—Dawn Freshwater, RGN, PhD, BA, RNT, FRCN
Reflections on Nursing Leadership

MAY 3

Authentic leaders exemplify the link between purpose and passion by
demonstrating congruence between their beliefs and actions.

—Maria R. Shirey, RN, MS, MBA, FACHE, CNAA, BC
Reflections on Nursing Leadership

MAY 4

The purpose of futures work is to study potential developments, using tools and certain attitudinal alignments, to effect change in a desired direction. A deliberated future may be personal, professional or organizational, but the process is the same: creating an image of a desired result to serve as a blueprint for action.

—Nancy Dickenson-Hazard, RN, MSN, FAAN
Reflections on Nursing Leadership

MAY 5

Remember what brought you to the profession of nursing. Make a conscious decision that you will seek a leadership role with the goal of finding order in the chaos that mires healthcare and nursing today.

—Beth Houser, RN, DNSc, FNP-C, CNAA, and Kathy Player, RN, EdD
Reflections on Nursing Leadership

MAY 6

The mentor hears the personality that speaks aloud and the soul that whispers in silence. Through this deep listening, the mentor can engage in a dialogue with the parts of the protégé's soul that have been kept in silence. When the protégé speaks with the voice of doubt, the mentor engages the voice of knowing. When the protégé speaks with the voice of fear, the mentor engages the voice of courage.

—Eric Klein, BA, and Nancy Dickenson-Hazard, RN, MSN, FAAN
Reflections on Nursing Leadership

MAY 7

She [Kirstin Stallknecht] learned to measure success in small increments. The path of reaching her goal was more important than the speed of getting to the finish line.

—Beth Houser, RN, DNSc, FNP-C, CNAA, and Kathy Player, RN, EdD
Pivotal Moments in Nursing, Volume II

MAY 8

We cannot understate the important role that strong, effective leaders have had in changing the status quo [in Mexico]. These nurse-leaders are determined and have the clear vision to overcome the slow-moving inertia of the system, the professional prejudice against nurses, and the hegemonic influence that some professionals use to control the decision-making process. ... For those of us who have participated in the creation of postgraduate nursing curricula in Mexico, it is our expectation that the strategies and actions that have been and are being slowly and progressively taken, will construct solid platforms for the professional development of nursing.

—Laura Morán Peña, RN, EdM
Reflections on Nursing Leadership

MAY 9

How people die remains in the memory of those who live on.

—Dame Cicely Saunders, OM, DBE
Founder of the modern hospice movement

MAY 10

The ability to see incongruities in life, to notice the incredible mismatches between what is and what ought to be is to know joy. I have a deep appreciation for the paradoxical nature of the life we have on this planet.

—Grayce Sills, RN, PhD
Pivotal Moments in Nursing, Volume II

MAY 11

The mentor spends time, energy, and professional capital to advance the protégé and is equally demanding that the protégé produce. If the relationship is successful, it will last until the protégé is ready to move on. And moving on must occur, although friendship and mutual respect may last a lifetime.

—Lucie S. Kelly, RN, PhD, FAAN
Reflections on Nursing Leadership

MAY 12

No man, not even a doctor, ever gives any other definition of what a nurse should be than this—"devoted and obedient." This definition would do just as well for a porter. It might even do for a horse. It would not do for a policeman.
[1859]

—Florence Nightingale

MAY 13

It takes courage to place yourself in someone else's space for two straight days, equal courage to invite them into yours, and even more courage to come prepared for the open and honest interactions necessary for meaningful results. One runs the risk that ideas and feelings will be rejected when taking such a chance, but unless we extend ourselves in these ways, we will miss the opportunity to realize our full potential.

—Jennifer L. Hobbs, RN, BSN
Reflections on Nursing Leadership

MAY 14

Linda [Aiken] is a risk taker who thrives on being told something is impossible. She is gifted in making the impossible look ordinary. She has taken the perspective of nursing to some of the most influential healthcare forums in the world because she is a nurse first.

—Beth Houser, RN, DNSc, FNP-C, CNAA, and Kathy Player, RN, EdD
Pivotal Moments in Nursing, Volume I

MAY 15

Leadership is the process of giving direction and facilitating the alignment of purpose, people, plans, and actions with the aim of serving a value-driven, co-created, desired outcome.

—Daniel J. Pesut, APRN, BC, PhD, FAAN
Contemporary Issues in Nursing, Volume II

MAY 16

People never outgrow their need for help, learning, and affirmation. The mentoring relationship encourages those involved to define and help themselves. It empowers and expands the soul and mind. It brings possibilities and potential into focus.

—Eric Klein, BA, and Nancy Dickerson-Hazard, RN, MSN, FAAN
Reflections on Nursing Leadership

MAY 17

Assisting students to develop reflection and self-evaluation skills may facilitate their movement along the novice to expert continuum.

—Diane L. Stuenkel, RN, MS
The HeART of Nursing, Second Edition

MAY 18

We're amazingly conservative. Now we can't be conservative anymore, because this is the [nursing] shortage to end all shortages. This is permanent.

—Melanie C. Dreher, RN, PhD, FAAN
Quote...end quote

MAY 19

Becoming influential opens doors to effect today's opportunities and tomorrow's challenges. Having the ability to present your ideas and have them listened to enables you to affect outcomes for your patients, your organizations, and for yourself.

—Eleanor Sullivan, RN, PhD, FAAN
Taking the Mystery Out of Influence

MAY 20

Nurses must risk—risk innovation; risk the frontiers of imagination and thought; risk being accountable for improving healthcare. Our successes will be realized only through taking risks, being tolerant of failure, and learning from those failures. If a lesson is learned, there really is no failure.

—Kathleen R. Stevens, RN, EdD, FAAN
Reflections on Nursing Leadership

MAY 21

A variety of effects of leadership on individuals and groups are possible, such as job satisfaction, empowerment, job performance, and retention. But ultimately a major institutional goal of leadership is to improve service to a client (in healthcare, the patient; in business, the customer) or the efficient and effective functioning of the organization itself.

—Connie Vance, RN, EdD, FAAN, and Elaine Larson, RN, PhD, FAAN
Journal of Nursing Scholarship

MAY 22

Nurse leaders, today and tomorrow, are accountable for necessary improvements in caring for patients and in caring for nurses. We have an obligation to both mankind and nurses.

—Judith Shamian, RN, PhD
Reflections on Nursing Leadership

MAY 23

The transition from being mentored to being a colleague is often very subtle and can happen at any time.

—Fay Bower, DNSc, FAAN
Building and Managing a Career in Nursing

MAY 24

It is nurses' time to lead—with confidence and the requisite skills.

—Susan B. Hassmiller, RN, PhD, FAAN
Reflections on Nursing Leadership

MAY 25

She [Vernice Ferguson] learned early on that no one discipline can solve all the problems of healthcare. Each discipline has unique gifts that it brings to the table. It was always Vernice's quest to be at the table. The one question she always asked, whether in her role as nurse leader of the VA medical center or chief nurse at the NIH, was "Where does the power lie?"

—Beth Houser, RN, DNSc, FNP-C, CNAA, and Kathy Player, RN, EdD
Pivotal Moments in Nursing, Volume I

MAY 26

You have to care about yourself first before you ever know how to care for another person. If you're going to deny you, you're certainly going to do the same thing for other people. That is not a good thing to do, to deny you.

—Clara Adams-Ender, RN, MSN, CNAA, FAAN
Reflections on Nursing Leadership

MAY 27

[Ada Sue Hinshaw] has commonly found herself in situations that were high pressure, chaotic, and uncontrolled. She has always responded by taking a deep breath and steadying herself, recognizing that she was representing the entire profession, not just herself. Ada Sue didn't mind taking risks, but she was always thinking of the consequences so that she could immediately begin the damage control.

—Beth Houser, RN, DNSc, FNP-C, CNAA, and Kathy Player, RN, EdD
Pivotal Moments in Nursing, Volume I

MAY 28

Creating communities is, without doubt, very hard work. In the process, we face cultural diversity, personal stereotypes, and inertial barriers that must be defeated. However, once work becomes fruitful, you feel satisfied for you have given of your ideals and capabilities, and you surely agree with what someone once stated, "To triumph in life is to lead others to their triumph."

—Laura Morán Peña, RN, EdM
Reflections on Nursing Leadership

MAY 29

Chaos is an essential constituent of all change. It works to unbundle attachment to whatever is impeding movement. Chaos challenges us to simultaneously let go and to take on. It reminds us that life is a journey of constant creation.

—Tim Porter-O'Grady, RN, PhD, FAAN, and Kathy Malloch, RN, MBA, PhD, FAAN
Quantum Leadership

MAY 30

Experience taught her [Rheba de Tornyay] that some of the best deans are those who are the best teachers. The best teachers are masters in group dynamics.

—Beth Houser, RN, DNSc, FNP-C, CNAA, and Kathy Player, RN, EdD
Pivotal Moments in Nursing, Volume I

Leadership is best attained through credibility over your actions and your integrity over time. It is not only talking the talk, but walking the walk.

—Richard Carmona, RN, MD, MPH, FACS
Pivotal Moments in Nursing, Volume II

June

JUNE 1

Nursing prepares you for excellence. Be proud you are a nurse.

—Ruth Lubic, CNM, EdD, FAAN, FACNM
First nurse to receive a MacArthur Fellowship "genius" grant
Pivotal Moments in Nursing, Volume II

JUNE 2

Twenty-first century leadership demands that leaders motivate and manage
movements to achieve lasting change. Leading a movement that effects change
requires a reflective practitioner and an individual willing to engage in a
constant critical dialogue with their practice.

—Dawn Freshwater, RGN, PhD, BA, RNT, FRCN
Reflections on Nursing Leadership

JUNE 3

Lesson #8: Be fair to yourself! Being a leader often means being subject to
scrutiny and critique. Leaders are natural targets for frustration, anger,
and blame. The challenge of being both responsive and, at the same time,
reasonably objective is enormous. Leaders must thoughtfully weigh input and
not be defeated or destroyed by it. This means that leaders need to develop
ways in which they can maintain a sense of balance and fairness in how they
see themselves and in what they do. Humility and humor are great allies in
this—as are friends and family who love you regardless of how bad a day you
had (having a dog isn't a bad idea either).

—Marla E. Salmon, RN, ScD, FAAN
Conversations With Leaders

JUNE 4

Positive leadership styles create lasting value that allows organizations and individuals to thrive over time.

—Maria R. Shirey, RN, MS, MBA, FACHE, CNAA, BC
Reflections on Nursing Leadership

JUNE 5

Young people will need support and nurturing to become tomorrow's nursing leaders. Who mentors them does make a difference. If they are mentored into a leadership style they do not admire or condone, they may seek other opportunities to lead outside nursing, such as in entrepreneurial opportunities or community-based organizational models.

—K. Lynn Wieck, RN, PhD, Margaret Prydun, RN, PhD, and Terri Walsh, RN, MS
Journal of Nursing Scholarship

JUNE 6

Communication forms the core of management activities and cuts across all phases of the management process.

—Bessie L. Marquis, RN, CNAA, MSN, and Carol J. Huston, RN, CNAA, MSN, DPA
Leadership Roles and Management Functions in Nursing, Fourth Edition

JUNE 7

A major aspect of the mentoring relationship is the mentor's ability to provide leadership. Leadership, in this sense, is being able to be futuristic, proactive, and yet grounded in reality.

—Fay L. Bower, DNSc, FAAN
Building and Managing a Career in Nursing

JUNE 8

Working with media and public relations is part of contemporary nursing leadership. By doing so, we add value to our work and that of our colleagues. Nursing leaders need to establish and maintain links to healthcare reporters.

—M. Colleen Stainton, RN, DNSs, FCN(NSW)
Reflections on Nursing Leadership

JUNE 9

If we are to adequately address challenges facing our own profession, ranging from shortage and recruitment to funding for nursing research, and if we the people are going to make strides in realigning our healthcare system, we must be at the table with policymakers. And we need to educate more nurses, through our organizations, about how to effectively get there.

—Mary Wakefield, RN, PhD
Reflections on Nursing Leadership

JUNE 10

Leaders must be open to the conversations around the controversy.

—Florence Schorske Wald, RN, MN, MS, FAAN
Pivotal Moments in Nursing, Volume II

JUNE 11

Centeredness is an inner strength—a sense of balance and depth. ...
Centeredness is an internal compass constructed from our individual values
and beliefs. ... Centeredness is a primary factor in servant leadership and
stewardship. It helps people find purpose in service and understand their need
to serve.

—Nancy Dickenson-Hazard, RN, MSN, FAAN
Reflections on Nursing Leadership

JUNE 12

[Loretta Ford's] military duty gave her ample opportunity to provide leadership
to the corpsmen with whom she worked, and she feels her military experience
infused a strong sense of discipline and teamwork which served her well
throughout her career.

—Beth Houser, RN, DNSc, FNP-C, CNAA, and Kathy Player, RN, EdD
Pivotal Moments in Nursing, Volume I

JUNE 13

Someone once said, "Leaders are people who develop leaders and not followers." This succinctly expresses the importance of succession planning.

—Roselin Ang, RN, MSN, and Long Chooi Fong, RN, MSc
Reflections on Nursing Leadership

JUNE 14

A large part of leadership is the ability to inspire passion and vision in others so that, together, everyone is working toward the same goal.

—Beth Houser, RN, DNSc, FNP-C, CNAA, and Kathy Player, RN, EdD
Reflections on Nursing Leadership

JUNE 15

In typical [Shirley Sears] Chater fashion, her strategic process allowed faculty and staff participation so ideas could be generated at all levels. She knew radical changes could not occur without ownership and buy-in from employees. ... In this instance, Shirley was able to use a crisis situation to organize a vision, a mission, and a set of objectives in order to guide the organization into the future, while still ensuring support from the employees.

—Beth Houser, RN, DNSc, FNP-C, CNAA, and Kathy Player, RN, EdD
Pivotal Moments in Nursing, Volume I

JUNE 16

Authentic leadership is the foundation of healthy work environments and the glue that holds those environments together.

—Maria R. Shirey, RN, MS, MBA, FACHE, CNAA, BC
Reflections on Nursing Leadership

JUNE 17

In times of uncertainty, complexity, and change, quality of leadership becomes increasingly important. History is replete with examples of positive leadership that have helped us effectively confront challenges and face the future with confidence, hope, optimism, and resiliency.

—Maria R. Shirey, RN, MS, MBA, FACHE, CNAA, BC
Reflections on Nursing Leadership

JUNE 18

As the mentoring journey is traversed, both protégé and mentor must determine priorities for achieving the dream. As the mentor advises and teaches, the protégé thoughtfully selects the best course of action. Along the way, the mentor praises a job well done and also provides support and solace when results are unfavorable.

—Eric Klein, BA, and Nancy Dickenson-Hazard, RN, MSN, FAAN
Reflections on Nursing Leadership

JUNE 19

For career development, the professional network is probably the best resource. After learning about an opportunity from a friend or work buddy, the best approach is to contact a member of the professional network who is the best source for accurate and up-to-date referral. For the development of a career, it is best to seek help from a professional network because it is these people who understand the rapidly changing healthcare scene.

—Fay L. Bower, DNSc, FAAN
Building and Managing a Career in Nursing

JUNE 20

Because of the hierarchical structure, the Chinese prefer leaders with great expertise and talents to behave as role models as well as to define clear tasks and goals for subordinates.

—Hsiu-Chin Chen, RN, PhD, EdD, Susan L. Beck, PhD, APRN, FAAN, and Linda K. Amos, RN, EdD, FAAN
Journal of Nursing Scholarship

JUNE 21

Career development is fundamentally about realizing our higher purpose and taking actions to make that purpose real in our organizations and our lives.

—Eric Klein, BA
Reflections on Nursing Leadership

JUNE 22

Stepping up to the challenge of leading others is nothing less than taking a risk and becoming vulnerable. Risk-taking is a wonderful way to stretch both personally and professionally to new limits. Stretching to the next rung on the leadership ladder is exchanging the autopilot of expert for the consciousness of novice.

—Beth Houser, RN, DNSc, FNP-C, CNAA, and Kathy Player, RN, EdD
Reflections on Nursing Leadership

JUNE 23

Trust people. They want what you want. They also want good outcomes.

—Gloria Smith, RN, PhD, FAAN
Conversations With Leaders

JUNE 24

Mentoring the emerging workforce as they begin to experiment with leadership roles is an excellent way to promote leadership behaviors.

—K. Lynn Wieck, RN, PhD, Margaret Prydun, RN, PhD, and Terri Walsh, RN, MS
Journal of Nursing Scholarship

JUNE 25

I know why I stay in nursing. My mentors showed me the way. They taught me how to competently care for patients, other nurses, and myself. I hope I have done the same for others. I want to mentor those who are trying to find their way, so they too will stay in nursing.

—Pamela R. Cangelosi, RNC, PhD
Reflections on Nursing Leadership

JUNE 26

By helping nurses connect their goals with the goals of the organization, the career coach supports the development of transformational leadership. .... Transformational leadership ... is the essential precursor of evidence-based management.

—Theresa L. Carroll, RN, PhD, and Tommye Austin, RN, MSN
Reflections on Nursing Leadership

JUNE 27

Leadership in the new age is leadership at the intersection. You think about leading your own discipline and doing all the things that help advance your discipline [that is] now moving to a new age where you have to lead interdisciplinary relationships, you have to teach people new roles, you have to be able to teach different relationships, you have to get to new agendas, you have to live in a value-based world rather than a volume-based world. All [of which] now redefine what leadership is and call us to a different place to learn it. Some of it we know, some of it we're learning as we go.

—Tim Porter-O'Grady, RN, PhD, FAAN
Contemporary Issues in Nursing, Volume II

JUNE 28

Nurses have a social responsibility to shape health-care policy, whether that policy affects national systems, organizations, health-care institutions, departments, units, corporations, or communities.

—Nancy Dickenson-Hazard, RN, MSN, FAAN
Reflections on Nursing Leadership

JUNE 29

We can only rekindle our spirit for nursing when we focus on our own healing and self care. Nursing takes a huge toll on us. With all the physical, emotional, and spiritual challenges we face daily, we cannot thrive in this profession without taking care of ourselves.

—Diane Sieg, RN, CLC
Reflections on Nursing Leadership

JUNE 30

In the mentoring relationship, the risks and expectations are many. Protégés are expected to perform and succeed, and mentors are expected to produce a following and develop the next generation. Both take risks and must work to discover potentials within themselves that permit growth, avoid over-dependency, and recognize when the relationship has achieved its goals. Success requires a balance between risk and outcome.

—Eric Klein, BA, and Nancy Dickerson-Hazard, RN, MSN, FAAN
Reflections on Nursing Leadership

July

JULY 1

The purpose of learning about the future is not to predict it but to understand the elements that shape it and to envision desirable circumstances so that progress can be made toward a preferred future rather than a catastrophic one.

—Nancy Dickenson-Hazard, RN, MSN, FAAN
Reflections on Nursing Leadership

JULY 2

We have the best sick-care system in the world. The problem is we don't have good health care.

—Jocelyn Elders, MD
Former surgeon general of the United States

JULY 3

For Faye [Abdellah], mentoring does not have to come from another nurse but could come from anyone. She believes leadership is leadership, and to choose a mentor outside of nursing can broaden an individual's perspective. An example Faye uses to illustrate the power of this kind of mentorship is Sister Rosemary Donley, former dean of the Catholic University of America School of Nursing. While serving as an intern in a senator's office, Sister Donley drafted successful hospice legislation that had a positive impact on the healthcare system. Sister Donley's ability to achieve this goal was, in part, the result of working closely as a mentee with the senator.

—Beth Houser, RN, DNSc, FNP-C, CNAA, and Kathy Player, RN, EdD
Pivotal Moments in Nursing, Volume I

JULY 4

All nurses are superheroes and are the foundation for healthcare in our nation and beyond.

—Katherine Kinsey, RN, PhD, FAAN
Conversations With Leaders

JULY 5

Power wins, not by being used, but by being there.

—Anonymous

JULY 6

Leaders move out into the unknown and, in doing so, challenge the process by which they, their constituents, and their organizations innovate, grow, and improve.

—Nancy Dickenson-Hazard, RN, MSN, FAAN
Reflections on Nursing Leadership

JULY 7

[The] most important thing for those in hierarchical positions is to fade into the background and let the others shine.

—Joyce Clifford, RN, PhD, FAAN
Pivotal Moments in Nursing, Volume I

JULY 8

It's easy to think that mentors are optimistic cheerleaders, forever reinforcing a positive mental attitude. But mentors understand the power of "no." ... Mentors recognize that in fulfilling one's destiny, saying "no" to the unnecessary is as important as saying "yes" to the dream.

—Eric Klein, BA, and Nancy Dickenson-Hazard, RN, MSN, FAAN
Reflections on Nursing Leadership

JULY 9

I see potential in students to lead and make a difference, and I tell them so, even if they can't see it in themselves yet.

—Carol A. Picard, RN, PhD
Reflections on Nursing Leadership

JULY 10

Effective nursing leaders are transformational not only in their management and leadership styles, but also in their very being. Not only are they advocates of critical reflection, they are living examples of reflection in and on action.

—Dawn Freshwater, RGN, PhD, BA, RNT, FRCN
Reflections on Nursing Leadership

JULY 11

Technology cannot replace leadership in setting the direction for our profession.

—Melanie C. Dreher, RN, PhD, FAAN
Reflections

JULY 12

Learning enables nurses to teach in a more meaningful way. The added bonus of learning while teaching is that what is learned goes into the individual collection of experiences, significantly enhancing wisdom in future teachings. In the end, all learn, all gain, and all realize that life's experiences haven't hurt us none.

—Nancy Dickenson-Hazard, RN, MSN, FAAN
Reflections on Nursing Leadership

JULY 13

To create a preferred future, each of us needs to consider what it means to be a navigator. A navigator is someone who has a destination in mind and adjusts course as needed.

—Daniel J. Pesut, APRN, BC, PhD, FAAN
Reflections on Nursing Leadership

JULY 14

Nurse managers set the tone, value, and work culture for the microsystems they lead. Staff migrate to microsystems that foster professional growth, professional nursing practice, data-based decision-making, and innovative practices, all of which are characteristics of cultures that promote adoption of evidence-based nursing practices.

—Marita G. Titler, RN, PhD, FAAN, Laura Cullen, RN, MA, and Gail Ardery, RN, PhD
Reflections on Nursing Leadership

JULY 15

Everything needs to be fed if it is to continue to grow and develop. Mentoring relationships thrive when a spirit of generativity and openness prevails. Life is an open classroom, and mentors and protégés who keep learning from each other fuel the fire.

—Eric Klein, BA, and Nancy Dickenson-Hazard, RN, MSN, FAAN
Reflections on Nursing Leadership

JULY 16

Gretta [Styles] learned early on in her career to be open to new opportunities and to take risks. What she lacked in experience during the early years, she more than made up for in courage. The option of failing in new ventures never crossed her mind. Gretta had become well rehearsed in life's early lessons of reaching for those things that appear beyond grasp.

—Beth Houser, RN, DNSc, FNP-C, CNAA, and Kathy Player, RN, EdD
Pivotal Moments in Nursing, Volume I

JULY 17

We don't have Florence Nightingale to share with us a vision of exactly what the solutions might be to unburden us and the people for whom we care. Nevertheless, we know that in very difficult times she exerted influence at both the bedside and in the halls of statesmen to craft solutions to the problems of her day. Her footprints are there. Will our organizations, through the work of each of us, follow them and, in the process, leave new footprints behind?

—Mary Wakefield, RN, PhD
Reflections on Nursing Leadership

JULY 18

Creating a well-rewarded and satisfying clinical career is of paramount importance, but to make it sufficiently robust requires clinical nurses to feel comfortable with research and their ability to offer their skills to others through teaching and modeling of expert behavior.

—Tony Butterworth, CBE, PhD, RMN, RGN, FRCN, FmedSci, FRCPsych
Reflections on Nursing Leadership

JULY 19

One male colleague who embraced what Faye [Glenn Abdellah] had to say was former Surgeon General C. Everett Koop. Dr. Koop and Fay worked closely together as a team for nine and a half years, with her in a position (deputy attorney general) that was never before held by a woman or a nurse. Dr. Koop and Faye were actively involved in the formation of national health policies related to AIDS, drug addiction, violence, smoking, and alcoholism. It was through their concerted efforts that smoking was banned on both domestic and, later, international flights.

—Beth Houser, RN, DNSc, FNP-C, CNAA, and Kathy Player, RN, EdD
Pivotal Moments in Nursing, Volume I

JULY 20

In this life we cannot do great things. We can only do small things with great love.

—Mother Theresa

JULY 21

It takes practice. One does not move from novice to expert—whether in stitching or nursing—in a flash...Reflection can help us learn from mistakes, identify strengths and weaknesses, and formulate an action plan for the future.

—Diane L. Stuenkel, RN, MS
The HeART of Nursing, Second Edition

JULY 22

Providing hands-on care for 24 hours a day, seven days a week has placed nurses in the unique position of gaining insights that can benefit the highest levels of leadership in hospitals. Nurses can offer substantive ideas about how care can be improved, how care environments might be safer, how the continuum of care might be smoother, how to better educate the next generation of students and, in general, how to create a better healthcare system for all.

—Susan B. Hassmiller, RN, PhD, FAAN
Reflections on Nursing Leadership

JULY 23

Managing relationships is a competency equivalent to clinical/technical and critical thinking. When these principles of healthy behavior are alive and visible within an organization, patients and their families are more likely to experience the fullness of a rich and rewarding connection to their nurse, which is also professionally satisfying for the nurse. A real win-win!

—Mary Koloroutis, RN, MS, and Jayne Felgen, RN, MPA
Reflections on Nursing Leadership

JULY 24

The mentor relationship is a contract. Being mentored by a non-nurse who has similar interests can enhance patient outcomes, as well as the protégé's own growth and development. Today, more than ever, nurses and other healthcare professionals must function as a team.

—Veronica Clarke-Tasker, RN, PhD, MBA
Reflections on Nursing Leadership

JULY 25

Mentoring is initiated every time nurses share experiences that exemplify the essence of nursing: the art of compassion. ... The art of nursing compassion rarely focuses on the cure alone, but rather on the process of bringing relief to an individual's pain and suffering. As with many arts, creating protégés requires cultivation and stimulation.

—Charlene Fullam, RN, MA, CEN
Reflections on Nursing Leadership

JULY 26

Those who are afraid to risk and fail never truly grow and reach their full potential. Even if I don't attain a goal, I still get satisfaction from the process and am able to learn something from the opportunity.

—Patricia E. Thompson, RN, EdD
Reflections on Nursing Leadership

JULY 27

Empowerment is a key to effective leadership.

—K. Lynn Wieck, RN, PhD, Margaret Prydun, RN, PhD, and Terri Walsh, RN, MS
Journal of Nursing Scholarship

JULY 28

Within us is a template or blueprint for our true nature—our core values, unique gifts, and chosen legacy. There is a part of us that remembers who we are, what we are here to learn, what wounds need healing and how we want to fully deploy our uniqueness. This part of us knows the contribution we most want to make through our lives. ... When we align our careers with this purpose, we become fully alive. We become ourselves. We become capable of the kind of leadership that is transformational.

—Eric Klein, BA
Reflections on Nursing Leadership

JULY 29

The first step toward becoming influential is to be able to understand what people *really* mean, regardless of their words or actions.

—Eleanor Sullivan, RN, PhD, FAAN
Taking the Mystery Out of Influence

JULY 30

Nurses have been exhorted to become research-based practitioners for many years in most of the world's advanced economies, but no research utilization initiative has explicated this in as clinically meaningful a way as the current international evidence-based, health-care movement

—Alan Pearson, RN, ONC, DipNED, DANS, MSc, PhD, FCN(NSW), FINA, FRCNA, FAAG, FRCN
Reflections on Nursing Leadership

Nursing needs its visionaries now! The world needs leaders in all walks of life who can work together, as a team, in order to bring about sustainability and collaboration. Nursing needs to be part of the team. We need to contribute to the production of the future, celebrate and manage change, and work in an open and democratic style. And we need to bring these attitudes, beliefs, and skills to the policy table.

—Iain Graham, RN, Med, MSc, PhD
Reflections on Nursing Leadership

Notes

August

AUGUST 1

I have always thought that the best sound in a hallway while at work is laughter. It means that people are taking pleasure in their work and in the company of their colleagues. Supporting such relationship building leads to creative strategies and solutions to challenges.

—Carol A. Picard, RN, PhD
Reflections on Nursing Leadership

AUGUST 2

[Linda Aiken's] leadership has been grounded in education, risk-taking, courage, patience, rigor, and, most prominently, vision.

—Beth Houser, RN, DNSc, FNP-C, CNAA, and Kathy Player, RN, EdD
Pivotal Moments in Nursing, Volume I

AUGUST 3

If you are a nurse, you can call yourself a leader ... each one of you! Whether you are a student nurse, a staff nurse, a nurse manager, or currently serving at the executive level, you are a leader.

—Susan B. Hassmiller, RN, PhD, FAAN
Reflections on Nursing Leadership

AUGUST 4

Reflecting over her career, [Gretta Styles] offers that it is much like the saying "build it and they will come," but with the twist of "make yourself an expert and people will find you." The key, as Gretta sees it, is "getting all the education you can, developing an expertise in particular areas, and then opportunity seeks you out."

—Beth Houser, RN, DNSc, FNP-C, CNAA, and Kathy Player, RN, EdD
Pivotal Moments in Nursing, Volume I

AUGUST 5

As leaders in nursing, we must mentor our students and new nurses. Only through our role modeling and mentoring will they decide to stay in nursing and find satisfaction in the multiple roles nursing has to offer. Maybe then the nursing shortage really will begin to ease.

—Pamela R. Cangelosi, RNC, PhD
Reflections on Nursing Leadership

AUGUST 6

Knowing when to change directions is a leadership skill developed through life's lessons, one that has been instrumental in guiding our profession. Florence Nightingale impacted mortality rates by improving sanitary conditions in hospitals during the 19th century. In 1965, Loretta Ford responded to the inadequate physician supply that threatened access to healthcare in America by heading up the nurse practitioner movement.

—Beth Houser, RN, DNSc, FNP-C, CNAA, and Kathy Player, RN, EdD
Reflections on Nursing Leadership

AUGUST 7

Nurses should develop skills that will help them be successful advocates and change agents. A few of these critical skills include effective communication, conflict resolution and negotiation. In addition, they should support each other. This is especially important for new graduates. New nurses need to be guided, encouraged and mentored.

—Patricia E. Thompson, RN, EdD
Reflections on Nursing Leadership

AUGUST 8

Develop your leadership skills, but remember that leadership isn't a job or a title. Leaders influence people and situations to bring about transforming change.

—International Leadership Institute
Honor Society of Nursing, Sigma Theta Tau International
Reflections on Nursing Leadership

AUGUST 9

All of us have been touched in some way by nursing's constancy in uncertain times. Without nurses, healing and restoration of health would surely be severely impaired. With them, humaneness and caring prevail.

—Nancy Dickenson-Hazard, RN, MSN, FAAN
Reflections on Nursing Leadership

AUGUST 10

You have to be enthusiastic and passionate about what you do…and, of course, excellent at what you do and what you believe, so it gets translated to other people.

—Vernice Ferguson, RN, MA, FAAN, FRCN
Pivotal Moments in Nursing, Volume I

AUGUST 11

Nursing is facing, once again, a choice for its future and it is important that it makes the right choice if it wishes to ensure that it serves the public and provides a healthcare system that is sustainable and equitable.

—Iain Graham, RN, Med, MSc, PhD
Reflections on Nursing Leadership

AUGUST 12

Leadership also calls for a drive to mentor and empower others.

—Susan B. Hassmiller, RN, PhD, FAAN
Reflections on Nursing Leadership

AUGUST 13

Protégés are intrigued by uncertainty, while mentors are inspired by the unknown. They know what fear is, without allowing the fear to dictate their choices. They don't push others over the edge alone. They readily join hands with people to leap into the future, confident in their collective ability to navigate the rapids of change.

—Eric Klein, BA, and Nancy Dickenson-Hazard, RN, MSN, FAAN
Reflections on Nursing Leadership

AUGUST 14

Nurses should use our organizational structures to press for conversation with elected officials. The challenges before us and the industry in which we work are too great for this profession to solve on its own, and too great to be solved without nursing's voice.

—Mary Wakefield, RN, PhD
Reflections on Nursing Leadership

AUGUST 15

Ada Sue [Hinshaw's] definition of "good people" are those colleagues who will complement not replicate strengths and who were willing to tell you "no." She believes leaders must listen carefully. The dissenting voice is the gift of a different perspective that could make all the difference.

—Beth Houser, RN, DNSc, FNP-C, CNAA, and Kathy Player, RN, EdD
Pivotal Moments in Nursing, Volume I

AUGUST 16

I believe the future of nursing rests heavily on present and future leaders, on those who are their followers, on nursing programs and on nursing organizations. I believe teaching and practicing leadership and followership characteristics by individuals and organizations are vital to our continued development as a profession.

—Billye Brown, RN, EdD, FAAN
Reflections on Nursing Leadership

AUGUST 17

Leaders understand that many have a stake in the vision and that achieving it requires others to have a sense of personal power, pride, and ownership.

—Nancy Dickenson-Hazard, RN, MSN, FAAN
Reflections on Nursing Leadership

AUGUST 18

A leader has to be sensitive to the people who are creative, to the people who are competitive, to the people who are into control, and to the people who are into collaboration.

—Daniel J. Pesut, APRN, BC, PhD, FAAN
Contemporary Issues in Nursing, Volume II

AUGUST 19

It is hard to imagine anyone wanting to be a mentor who did not have an interest in helping another learn and advance.

—Fay L. Bower, DNSc, FAAN
Building and Managing a Career in Nursing

AUGUST 20

Being a leader is not for sissies! Certainly the challenge of leadership is great. Sometimes, leadership is even dangerous. It takes self-knowing, strong beliefs, continual development of leadership qualities, and a set of tools ready for use at a moment's notice.

—Nancy Dickenson-Hazard, RN, MSN, FAAN
Reflections on Nursing Leadership

AUGUST 21

To speak about my relationship with Virginia Henderson, I am impelled to convey the broadest possible meaning for the term mentor. For me, Virginia was much more than the wise, experienced, trusted advisor, and advocate generally ascribed to this term.

—Rhetaugh Graves Dumas, RN, PhD, FAAN
Virginia Avenel Henderson: Signature for Nursing

AUGUST 22

It is the leader's responsibility to recognize the resistance or conflict.

—Florence Schorske Wald, RN, MN, MS, FAAN
Pivotal Moments in Nursing, Volume II

AUGUST 23

Learning should not be limited to the ideas of one. Diversity of thought is an essential element to professional expansion—one's own ego should not become a barrier when preparing the next generation of thought leaders.

—Florence Schorske Wald, RN, MN, MS, FAAN
Pivotal Moments in Nursing, Volume II

AUGUST 24

Leadership and management are equally important but, unlike management, leadership involves change. Since change is disruptive to an organization and can contribute to the organization's demise, it needs to be episodic rather than periodic.

—Barbara A. Trent, RN, EdD
Reflections on Nursing Leadership

AUGUST 25

Leadership is distinctly different from your substantive area of expertise or rank and requires core competencies. Being a good nurse or good doctor or good officer doesn't make one the best leader for all situations.

—Richard Carmona, RN, MD, MPH, FACS
Pivotal Moments in Nursing, Volume II

AUGUST 26

Thinking, learning, and acting strategically is a continuous developmental journey for leaders.

—Nancy Dickenson-Hazard, RN, MSN, FAAN
Reflections on Nursing Leadership

AUGUST 27

Acceptance is key to creating meaningful interactions among the four generations currently involved in nursing—acceptance that there are certain core values that each generation is working to foster in those around them and that they exemplify as healers and caregivers.

—Jennifer L. Hobbs, RN, BSN
Reflections on Nursing Leadership

AUGUST 28

I can think of no other profession that permits us to be heroes every day, to know as we go home after a day's work that we have made an extraordinary difference in the life of other humans.

—Melanie C. Dreher, RN, PhD, FAAN
Reflections on Nursing Leadership

AUGUST 29

I really feel, once a nurse, always a nurse, because if you have come up in that culture and you've had the opportunity of belonging to that unique fraternity, there is a certain way you see patients and you see care and you see life. To me, it very much complements who I became as a physician, and certainly I draw upon those skills every day as U.S. surgeon general.

—Richard Carmona, RN, MD, MPH, FACS
Reflections on Nursing Leadership

AUGUST 30

Servant leadership promotes service to others, a holistic approach to work, personal development, and shared decision-making. It also carries the responsibility of stewardship, of being the guardian of the balance between inner strength and action, and of acting in the best interest of those who are being served.

—Nancy Dickenson-Hazard, RN, MSN, FAAN
Reflections on Nursing Leadership

As nurses, we are oriented toward developing, empowering, and nurturing relationships, and we carry with us the potential for powerful mentoring.

—Jeanette Boman, RN, PhD
Reflections on Nursing Leadership

September

SEPTEMBER 1

Get to the table and be a player, or someone who does not understand nursing will do that for you.

—Loretta Ford, RN, EdD, PNP, FAAN, FAANP
Pivotal Moments in Nursing, Volume I

SEPTEMBER 2

Change is never accomplished alone, and incorporating the talents of the members of the group into an idea requires coordination and strategic planning. For her [Rheba de Tornyay], the ideal situation occurs when the idea comes back to the leader as an original group idea. Along the way, she has learned that patience supports this transition of ownership.

—Beth Houser, RN, DNSc, FNP-C, CNAA, and Kathy Player, RN, EdD
Pivotal Moments in Nursing, Volume I

SEPTEMBER 3

[Effective mentoring requires that] leaders recognize the value of their nurses and support an environment that encourages empowerment and growth. Second, senior nurses or mentors must recognize their capability to mentor and inspire new nurses. Finally, new nurses must be comfortable with the expectations of a mentoring relationship and be open to the bond that will inevitably develop.

—Charlene Fullam, RN, MA, CEN
Reflections on Nursing Leadership

SEPTEMBER 4

Reflection is learning from everyday experiences with the intent of realizing desirable practice. Through reflection, the practitioner gains insights into self and practice that can be applied either intuitively or deliberately in future situations, like seeds planted in the mind that germinate and bloom when the time is right.

—Christopher Johns, PhD
Reflections on Nursing Leadership

SEPTEMBER 5

The world of the 21st century will be an information/knowledge management world. Advancing knowledge and practice requires nursing to become more sensitive, too, and more skilled at dealing with all sorts of competing interests. The central role of nursing may be that of being a change agent. The choice to be made is whether nurses wish to be proactive or reactive to the changes.

—Iain Graham, RN, Med, MSc, PhD
Reflections on Nursing Leadership

SEPTEMBER 6

She [Joyce Clifford] learned a valuable leadership lesson—take advantage of opportunities because you never know where they might take you. ... She advises her mentees to, likewise, keep their eyes and ears open and seize the opportunities that come along.

—Beth Houser, RN, DNSc, FNP-C, CNAA, and Kathy Player, RN, EdD
Pivotal Moments in Nursing, Volume I

SEPTEMBER 7

To deliver the highest quality of care, nursing must accelerate its pace of translating research into practice. ... Most important are that a clear vision, strong belief, teamwork, and persistence are essential elements for success.

—Bernadette Mazurek Melnyk, RN, PhD, CPNP/NPP, FAAN, FNAP, and Ellen Fineout-Overholt, RN, PhD
Reflections on Nursing Leadership

SEPTEMBER 8

In order to stay grounded, it is important that healthcare leaders stay in close contact with patients.

—Leah Curtin, RN, DSc, MS, MA, FAAN
Pivotal Moments in Nursing, Volume II

SEPTEMBER 9

The quality of your work life is in large measure determined in your head. An optimist will look for ways to succeed and recognize that when a horse dies, it's time to get off. Don't complain, just take action.

—Brenda L. Lyon, RN, DNS, FAAN
Reflections on Nursing Leadership

SEPTEMBER 10

Encouraging our students to develop time management skills, pay attention to details, and to think creatively will serve them well as nurses and as life-long learners.

—Diane L. Stuenkel, RN, MS
The HeART of Nursing, Second Edition

SEPTEMBER 11

Whether it's disaster caused by terrorism or individual crisis caused by illness, nurses are present to heal trauma and assuage fear, confusion, uncertainty and pain. ... Oftentimes it's not what we say or do, but our presence that counts.

—Janice Post-White, RN, PhD, FAAN
Reflections on Nursing Leadership

SEPTEMBER 12

Leadership does not reside exclusively in people with high-level titles.

—Pat Thompson, RN, EdD
Reflecting on 30 Years of Nursing Leadership: 1975-2005

SEPTEMBER 13

Colleagues describe Ada Sue [Hinshaw's] leadership as the "total package" because she has the ability to bring the players to the table and address formidable issues. She is a consensus builder who has developed the fine art of merging the leadership mission from multiple disciplines so they can work collaboratively.

—Beth Houser, RN, DNSc, FNP-C, CNAA, and Kathy Player, RN, EdD
Pivotal Moments in Nursing, Volume I

SEPTEMBER 14

Delegation is not an option for the manager—it is a necessity.

—Bessie L. Marquis, RN, CNAA, MSN, and Carol J. Huston, RN, CNAA, MSN, DPA
Leadership Roles and Management Functions in Nursing, Fourth Edition

SEPTEMBER 15

Discussing expectations and determining what is doable help prevent anxiety, irritation, or anger.

—Brenda L. Lyon, RN, DNS, FAAN
Reflections on Nursing Leadership

SEPTEMBER 16

Authentic leaders value relationship building. They establish connections with others through their ability to share life stories, develop trust and intimacy, and cultivate community.

—Maria R. Shirey, RN, MS, MBA, FACHE, CNAA, BC
Reflections on Nursing Leadership

SEPTEMBER 17

A mentoring relationship fans the flame of passions and dreams. It stimulates self-esteem and self-confidence and contributes to personal and professional satisfaction.

—Eric Klein, BA, and Nancy Dickenson-Hazard, RN, MSN, FAAN
Reflections on Nursing Leadership

SEPTEMBER 18

We must, for the sake of our profession, be smart about who we are and where we are going. The generations currently at work in nursing have the chance to take a proactive rather than reactive approach to preparing the next generation of leaders.

—Jennifer L. Hobbs, RN, BSN
Reflections on Nursing Leadership

SEPTEMBER 19

To make use of their insights about improving care, nurses need to have their voices heard. Whether on the boards of healthcare organizations, serving as unit managers, or teaching in schools of nursing, nurses must first develop skills to communicate their visions. Second, to turn vision into action, they must learn to plan strategically.

—Susan B. Hassmiller, RN, PhD, FAAN
Reflections on Nursing Leadership

SEPTEMBER 20

Rheba [de Tornyay] also learned the art of reflection. This was a strategy she employed early in her leadership development, in which she would ask how the situation had gone and what she could have done differently. Remaining focused on the goals allowed Rheba to move through difficult situations with confidence and determination.

—Beth Houser, RN, DNSc, FNP-C, CNAA, and Kathy Player, RN, EdD
Pivotal Moments in Nursing, Volume I

SEPTEMBER 21

Mentors often see the future that is hidden in another's personality and abilities. ... Like a forest that grows from a single seed, mentors recognize that by nurturing one person's life, they will affect the lives of many.

—Eric Klein, BA, and Nancy Dickenson-Hazard, RN, MSN, FAAN
Reflections on Nursing Leadership

SEPTEMBER 22

Each nurse has to look not just at "a day's work," but at what he or she is investing in the future of the profession.

—Mary Woody, RN, MA, FAAN
Reflections on Nursing Leadership

SEPTEMBER 23

Apprehension, uncertainty, waiting, expectation, fear of surprise, do a patient more harm than any exertion.

—Florence Nightingale

SEPTEMBER 24

Working together as nurses and midwives at a global level is essential if we are to make a difference in the quality of life of the communities and individuals we serve. ... We empower ourselves when we work together.

—Barbara A. Parfitt, RGN, RM, FNP, PhD
Reflections on Nursing Leadershipp

SEPTEMBER 25

Leadership requires the use of power resources that are built upon expertise and knowledge. Based on their education and experience, all nurses have resources that can be refined and expanded upon to facilitate and effect change. These skills are within our capacity and are not limited to only a few individuals.

—Barbara A. Trent, RN, EdD
Reflections on Nursing Leadership

SEPTEMBER 26

A leader takes people where they want to go. A great leader takes people where they don't necessarily want to go, but ought to be.

—Rosalynn Carter

SEPTEMBER 27

There is no monitor or automated voice or robotic equipment that can comfort a dying patient or console a family member.

—Melanie C. Dreher, RN, PhD, FAAN
Reflections on Nursing Leadership

SEPTEMBER 28

It is the responsibility of leaders to use authority to create a vision for the future that benefits the profession.

—Angela Barron McBride, RN, PhD, FAAN
Orchestrating a faculty career.
Presentation in Leadership in Complex Systems

SEPTEMBER 29

As the recruitment and retention crisis expands, the nursing profession must activate its ethos of caring through strengthening mentor connections at every level in the profession. This is no longer just an option, but a necessity.

—Connie Vance, RN, EdD, FAAN
Reflections on Nursing Leadership

SEPTEMBER 30

I have found in life one must be visible in fighting for what one is passionate about, and hope the rest will follow.

—Claire Fagin, RN, PhD, FAAN
Pivotal Moments in Nursing, Volume I

Notes

October

OCTOBER 1

All nurses possess the ability to mentor and all have the power to institute change. Mentoring allows nurses to give back to the profession by answering the call to leadership.

—Theresa A. Granger, MN, ARNP, NP-C
Reflections on Nursing Leadership

OCTOBER 2

It is important to know that you need a lot of help when moving an agenda forward, and you can't afford to make enemies.

—Ruth Lubic, CNM, EdD, FAAN, FACNM
First nurse to receive a MacArthur Fellowship "genius" grant
Pivotal Moments in Nursing, Volume II

OCTOBER 3

Any attempt to bridge the generational gap requires open-mindedness and a certain amount of trust that each generation is acting, within its own context, for the good of the whole. The most important thing to realize about being open-minded is that it usually requires more listening and observing than talking.

—Jennifer L. Hobbs, RN, BSN
Reflections on Nursing Leadership

OCTOBER 4

Recognize the talent of others and acknowledge it.

—Gloria Smith, RN, PhD, FAAN
Conversations With Leaders

OCTOBER 5

Through relationships, I learned about different perspectives, about diversity in interpretations, about the meaning of multiculturalism, and about empowerment to achieve goals and realize dreams.

—Afaf Meleis, RN, PhD, FAAN
Conversations With Leaders

OCTOBER 6

Authentic leaders practice self-discipline by incorporating balance into their personal and professional lives.

—Maria R. Shirey, RN, MS, MBA, FACHE, CNAA, BC
Reflections on Nursing Leadership

OCTOBER 7

People who tell you to focus on your weaknesses have it all wrong, because you can only make marginal progress in this category. Your strengths are your natural talents that form the basis of your leadership style.

—Margaret McClure, RN, PhD, FAAN
Pivotal Moments in Nursing, Volume II

OCTOBER 8

Influential leaders know how to admit errors, correct them the best they can, and move on.

—Eleanor Sullivan, RN, PhD, FAAN
The Rules of the Game

OCTOBER 9

You can't go anywhere without leaving somewhere.

—Marla Salmon, RN, ScD, FAAN
Pivotal Moments in Nursing, Volume II

OCTOBER 10

Taking a risk means the unwarranted fear that keeps nurses from taking the lead must be removed. Mark Twain once said, "I have had a great many troubles, but most of them never happened." Like Twain, nurses need to take reasonable precautions but not let their worries and fears direct their actions.

—Fay L. Bower, DNSc, FAAN
Nurses Taking the Lead

OCTOBER 11

He [Richard Carmona] knows that a warm hug, handshake, hand holding, or eye-to-eye contact are methods to communicate human caring beyond the provision of healthcare.

—Beth Houser, RN, DNSc, FNP-C, CNAA, and Kathy Player, RN, EdD
Pivotal Moments in Nursing, Volume II

OCTOBER 12

Showing appreciation and creating a culture of celebration are serious business for a leader. ... Regardless of the method, leaders must promote encouragement in visible ways and, through action, link appreciation to performance.

—Nancy Dickenson-Hazard, RN, MSN, FAAN
Reflections on Nursing Leadership

OCTOBER 13

Become a global citizen, traveling and learning about the world's cultures. Assess your talents and skills. Explore varied workplaces and roles where you can develop to the fullest.

—International Leadership Institute
Honor Society of Nursing, Sigma Theta Tau International
Reflections on Nursing Leadership

OCTOBER 14

To have nurses be actualized through my office, my resources, and through me, so they could continue to grow and be whatever they wanted to be in nursing, is just one of the ways of giving back.

—Vernice Ferguson, RN, MA, FAAN, FRCN
Pivotal Moments in Nursing, Volume I

OCTOBER 15

What then is power? Power is the ability to influence who, what, when, where, and how things get accomplished. Think about the need for power, the scope of power, the extension of power, in its relationship to leadership. Think about the economics of power, the costs of power (psychological and financial), and the opportunities afforded by power. In this context, the ingredients for power must consist of desire, broad thinking, possession of some form of capital (be it money or an asset such as education), the ability to sacrifice, and on occasion, neurotic behavior.

—Barbara Nichols, RN, DHL, MS, FAAN
Conversations With Leaders

OCTOBER 16

There is a wonderful moment in the story *Alice's Adventures in Wonderland* by Lewis Carroll when there is a choice to make about direction. There are two roads, and Alice asks the Cheshire Cat which direction she should take. This question is met with the response, "That depends a good deal on where you want to get to." "I don't much care where," answered Alice. To that, the Cheshire Cat's response was, "Then it doesn't matter which way you go."

—Salvatore Tagliareni, PhD
Conversations With Leaders

OCTOBER 17

A great need exists for research focused on how leadership makes a difference in outcomes, such as quality patient care and improvements in organizational quality and productivity.

—Connie Vance, RN, EdD, FAAN, and Elaine Larson, RN, PhD, FAAN, CIC
Journal of Nursing Scholarship

OCTOBER 18

E-mentoring requires efficient electronic communication modes that quickly bridge substantial distances and time zones. ... Personal connections and personal responsibility are hallmarks for E-mentoring as much as for traditional mentoring.

—Mary W. Byrne, MPH, PhD, CPNP, and Maureen R. Keefe, RN, PhD, FAAN
Journal of Nursing Scholarship

OCTOBER 19

Life is a bunch of trade-offs and at the end of the day, you will not be able to accomplish everything you may have hoped or dreamed of, but if you are true to yourself, you will feel good about your choices and the tradeoffs you had to make.

—Jane Eisner
Conversations With Leaders

OCTOBER 20

Denmark is such a small country that the people do not need to use their resources to create new processes and systems, but they do need to learn and take from the best of what other countries have found effective. This influence is also part of how Kirsten [Stallknecht] approaches leadership and change. Instead of approaching situations thinking she has all the answers, she listens first to what ideas others have to offer and applies the best to her own situation.

—Beth Houser, RN, DNSc, FNP-C, CNAA, and Kathy Player, RN, EdD
Pivotal Moments in Nursing, Volume II

OCTOBER 21

Orders should not just flow from the top down, without considering those who have the hands-on, day-to-day experiences of working with the patients and their families.

—Vernice Ferguson, RN, MA, FAAN, FRCN
Pivotal Moments in Nursing, Volume I

OCTOBER 22

[Faye Glenn Abdellah] learned from her failures that it is very difficult to change the behavior of others. She resolved that one has to find what she calls a "hook" in order to drive behavior to change. ... She was never effective in stopping teen smoking habits until she found her hook. After numerous attempts at educating teens (particularly girls) against smoking, she found the ammunition she needed to make the difference. An article in the *New England Journal of Medicine* documented that smoking in young girls causes premature wrinkles. She went back to high schools and shared this perspective and was greeted with comments like, "Why didn't you tell us that in the first place?"

—Beth Houser, RN, DNSc, FNP-C, CNAA, and Kathy Player, RN, EdD
Pivotal Moments in Nursing, Volume I

OCTOBER 23

She [Virginia Henderson] was always able to see seeds of wisdom in colleagues' and students' minds, and she publicly and privately inspired, encouraged, and facilitated the blossoming of ideas into visions of leadership and improved patient care.

—Judith B. Kauss, RN, MSN, FAAN
Virginia Avenel Henderson: Signature for Nursing

OCTOBER 24

At different points in time throughout the leadership process, contingent upon an individual's power resources, leaders will serve as collaborators and collaborators will serve as leaders. In other words, leaders and collaborators interchangeably utilize their power resources to attract or entice others to join their group in order to bring about a change that reflects their mutual purposes.

—Barbara A. Trent, RN, EdD
Reflections on Nursing Leadership

OCTOBER 25

It is my hope that nurses who care for patients in diverse cultures will develop their own nursing theories. Such theories will help nurses deliver personalized care that is sensitive to the patient's cultural context. In turn, this helps nurses recognize their own critical legacies as practitioners of a scientific, humanistic healing art.

—Kay Keiko Hisama, RN, PhD
Reflections on Nursing Leadership

OCTOBER 26

If senior nurses will acknowledge the responsibility of mentorship and will encourage rather than discourage young nurses, they can be a powerful influence and a key to a successful staff and workplace.

—Charlene Fullam, RN, MA, CEN
Reflections on Nursing Leadership

OCTOBER 27

It is widely recognized that working alongside knowledgeable and respected mentors kindles enthusiasm and commitment to learning, promotes curiosity and critical thinking, and enhances self-confidence. ... A positive experience of mentored research motivates mentees to acquire more research skills through formal research training.

—Genevieve Gray, RN, MSc (Nursing), Dip Adv Nurs Studs, Dip Ned, CM, FRCNA, FCN(NSW)
Reflections on Nursing Leadership

OCTOBER 28

It is said that we teach what we most need to learn. It is important that, as nurses, we model to our patients' ways of being healthy. Thus, the practitioner is urged to attend to their own physical, psychological, emotional, and spiritual needs.

—Dawn Freshwater, RGN, PhD, BA, RNT, FRCN
Reflections on Nursing Leadership

OCTOBER 29

Every crisis offers opportunity, and the current nursing shortage is no exception. For nurses wanting to take the leap into a leadership position, the timing has never been better.

—Beth Houser, RN, DNSc, FNP-C, CNAA, and Kathy Player, RN, EdD
Reflections on Nursing Leadershipp

OCTOBER 30

Mentors are able to observe events as they are, without adding their own emotional interpretations and judgments. ... Because of their deep acceptance of life as it is, mentors can help protégés to see themselves as they are and to accept their own strengths and weaknesses. In turn, protégés enable mentors to see themselves.

—Eric Klein, BA, and Nancy Dickenson-Hazard, RN, MSN, FAAN
Reflections on Nursing Leadership

OCTOBER 31

Leaders must be aware of their strengths, their weaknesses, and the obstacles that keep them from exercising their ability to lead. They must be able to let go of personal agendas, become a member of the team, and use their abilities to help the team achieve their desired outcomes.

—Fay L. Bower, DNSc, FAAN
Nurses Taking the Lead

Notes

November

NOVEMBER 1

The survival of nursing depends on our ability to shape leaders who will work to unite the profession.

—Theresa A. Granger, MN, ARNP, NP-C
Reflections on Nursing Leadership

NOVEMBER 2

Authentic leadership is positive leadership practiced by individuals who are genuine, trustworthy, reliable, and believable.

—Maria R. Shirey, RN, MS, MBA, FACHE, CNAA, BC
Reflections on Nursing Leadership

NOVEMBER 3

Good leadership is a conscious enterprise—all that you think, envision, decide, and do are guided at some level by what you believe a leader is and does.

—Marla Salmon, RN, ScD, FAAN
Conversations With Leaders

NOVEMBER 4

It is easy to be pulled toward conformity or the status quo, to "fit in," to be "normal," to gain "acceptance" by the dominant framework. Thus nursing often has pursued conforming to what is, or catching up with the dominant paradigm, rather than sustaining its timeless dimensions and envisioning what might be. ... However, we are still in a place in time and space between our evolution and awakening in which we still have to learn about ourselves and our own power *with*, not *over*, another person, another nation, another culture, another nationality, and another's values. And on it goes.

—Jean Watson, RN, PhD, HNC, FAAN
Conversations With Leaders

NOVEMBER 5

Joyce [Clifford] was gifted at being able to present the vision and then get out of the way and let those with the most knowledge create the reality.

—Beth Houser, RN, DNSc, FNP-C, CNAA, and Kathy Player, RN, EdD
Pivotal Moments in Nursing, Volume I

NOVEMBER 6

If you're not part of the problem, you're part of the solution.

—Unknown

NOVEMBER 7

It is said that we teach what we most need to learn. It is important that, as nurses, we model to our patients' ways of being healthy. Thus, the practitioner is urged to attend to their own physical, psychological, emotional, and spiritual needs.

—Dawn Freshwater, RGN, PhD, BA, RNT, FRCN
Reflections on Nursing Leadership

NOVEMBER 8

A savvy game player learns the rules and uses them to accomplish goals, deal with problems, and build a satisfying career. Nurses, unaware of the game of work and the rules that control the game, inhibit their ability to influence their environment and that of their patients.

—Eleanor Sullivan, RN, PhD, FAAN
The Rules of the Game

NOVEMBER 9

Other than marriage, mentor relationships are probably the closest, most intimate, and most helpful relationships one can be part of.

—Fay L. Bower, DNSc, FAAN
Building and Managing a Career in Nursing

NOVEMBER 10

Political fundraisers are not just for the rich and famous. If you cannot afford to go to the big five-figure receptions and dinners, find a way to register guests or collect the money so you can still be there. This is a big issue in the nursing field. Despite being the largest healthcare profession, with more than 2.8 million nurses, nurses are still not acknowledged as partners by many medical and political counterparts. Partially, this is due to nurses not attending the right, visible fundraisers where presence means everything.

—Colleen Conway-Welch, RN, PhD, FAAN
Conversations With Leaders

NOVEMBER 11

Leadership takes place in a context, and it is the ability to keep and maintain a positive context that makes those around us want to stay engaged.

—Terry Fulmer, RN, PhD, FAAN
Conversations With Leaders

NOVEMBER 12

Get to know the political process. It is a dance and requires persistence and patience.

—Tine Hansen-Turton, MGA
Conversations With Leaders

NOVEMBER 13

The path to long-lasting life satisfaction starts with a sustainable pace. Striking a healthy balance between work time and leisure time provides the human body and mind with the required restorative maintenance needed to be able to operate at top capacity.

—Barbara Ann D'Anna, RN, MSN, CNOR
Reflections on Nursing Leadership

NOVEMBER 14

Nurses need to believe in themselves and believe in a future that they can make different from the present and the past.

—Iain Graham, RN, MEd, MSc, PhD
Reflections on Nursing Leadership

NOVEMBER 15

Operationalizing vision is the responsibility of the leader.

—Marla Salmon, RN, ScD, FAAN
Pivotal Moments in Nursing, Volume II

NOVEMBER 16

One of the critical aspects of the exchange phase is the mentor's and protégé's abilities to communicate honestly. This means both parties must be able to offer and accept criticism and to truthfully dialogue. There are times when things do not go smoothly or advice did not pay off. The mentor and the protégé must be willing and able to deal with what occurs, good or bad, and to seek solutions that benefit both individuals.

—Fay L. Bower, DNSc, FAAN
Building and Managing a Career in Nursing

NOVEMBER 17

Joyce [Clifford] built a career by empowering nurses, capitalizing on knowledge, applying accountability to clinical practice, and developing leaders at all levels.

—Beth Houser, RN, DNSc, FNP-C, CNAA, and Kathy Player, RN, EdD
Pivotal Moments in Nursing, Volume I

NOVEMBER 18

Challenging the process requires the leader to deliver disturbing news, raise difficult questions, and prod people to take on something new.

—Nancy Dickenson-Hazard, RN, MSN, FAAN
Reflections on Nursing Leadership

NOVEMBER 19

Nurses' opinions are being sought, and nurses are speaking out about what actions can be taken both within and outside of healthcare to mitigate the nursing shortage. We need to take this opportunity to speak clearly on this issue but also on the many others that are adversely impacting the healthcare of the public.

—Mary Wakefield, RN, PhD
Reflections on Nursing Leadership

NOVEMBER 20

We felt that these nursing leadership stories had to be told. We feel that the future of nursing depends on our ability to understand the past through the profound leadership lessons we can learn from those who have gone before us. We wanted to share how these leaders were ordinary people who have accomplished extraordinary outcomes in their careers, and in turn, we hope to inspire future leaders to envision their own leadership capacities through a richer understanding of these leaders and how their respective journeys evolved—warts and all.

—Beth Houser, RN, DNSc, FNP-C, CNAA, and Kathy Player, RN, EdD
Pivotal Moments in Nursing, Volume I

NOVEMBER 21

Being a feminist, defined by me as a person concerned both with personal development *and* the welfare of others (family, colleagues, patients, etc.) has energized me in many ways, from imagining new career possibilities for myself and developing mentoring structures for the next generation to changing how my university saw the school of nursing and how our hospital network valued nurses. Wearing that feminist label, I would like to think that I have addressed yin and yang simultaneously, drawing attention to both the importance of nursing's invaluable maintenance work and nursing's role in exerting the transformational leadership required for healthcare to achieve its preferred future.

—Angela Barron McBride, RN, PhD, FAAN
Conversations With Leaders

NOVEMBER 22

Please think about leadership and politics. Think about how this relates to race, age, sex, power, leadership, mentoring, conflict, organizational politics, pressures, and influence. Think about Darwin's theory—the fittest survive.

—Barbara Nichols, RN, DHL, MS, FAAN
Conversations With Leaders

NOVEMBER 23

When assessing how far nursing practice has progressed within a country, Gretta [Styles] essentially used two criteria:

1. Look at the educational requirement and the development of higher education, and

2. Assess the leadership positions in the government held by nurses.

—Beth Houser, RN, DNSc, FNP-C, CNAA, and Kathy Player, RN, EdD
Pivotal Moments in Nursing, Volume I

NOVEMBER 24

No one else can steal your talent.

—Gloria Smith, RN, PhD, FAAN
Conversations With Leaders

NOVEMBER 25

Leadership is essentially a work in progress—a never-ending journey with facets and elements that add up to a broad and complex mosaic.

—Tim Porter-O'Grady, RN, PhD, FAAN, and Kathy Malloch, RN, MBA, PhD, FAAN
Quantum Leadership

NOVEMBER 26

Healthcare leaders must focus on creating work cultures within which people feel connected, seen, supported, where they know they can count on each other and are in this together. Leaders need to lift up the value and significance of relationships—to self, to co-workers, to patients, and families.

—Mary Koloroutis, RN, MS, and Jayne Felgen, RN, MPA
Reflections on Nursing Leadership

NOVEMBER 27

Inspiring shared vision requires people to think differently, experiment, discover and change. If a leader fails to clearly articulate vision and blend it with reality, people will not be able to recognize their contributions and realize they are making a difference.

—Nancy Dickenson-Hazard, RN, MSN, FAAN
Reflections on Nursing Leadership

NOVEMBER 28

Career coaching is about matching the goals and resources of the organization with the goals and strengths of individual employees. When this is done effectively, both the individual and the organization achieve positive outcomes (Schein, 1978).

—Theresa L. Carroll, RN, PhD, and Tommye Austin, RN, MSN
Reflections on Nursing Leadership

NOVEMBER 29

The wise leader should think through who would be opposed and why and carefully prepare the response.

—Margaret McClure, RN, PhD, FAAN
Pivotal Moments in Nursing, Volume II

NOVEMBER 30

Leaders need to express appreciation authentically, in ways that appeal to individual passions, beliefs and dreams. When leaders encourage in this way—by connecting vision to action—they build a sense of collective identity and community.

—Nancy Dickenson-Hazard, RN, MSN, FAAN
Reflections on Nursing Leadership

Notes

December

DECEMBER 1

The best leaders are those who are empowered by the people they lead.

—Richard Carmona, RN, MD, MPH, FACS
Pivotal Moments in Nursing, Volume II

DECEMBER 2

In the same way I learned to celebrate my place in life after developing a personal vision, I learned to celebrate nursing after developing a vision to guide my nursing practice. When I fall short of the ideals outlined in my personal nursing vision, I don't view it as failure because it still pushes me to strive and achieve more than I would without a vision.

—Shawna Beese-Bjurstrom, RN, BSN, C, CCRN
Reflections on Nursing Leadership

DECEMBER 3

The practical application of generational strengths in any organization begins with cooperative structuring of leadership roles to include job sharing and mentoring, and it is vital that as much importance be placed on the support of new leaders as is placed on the leadership role itself.

—Jennifer L. Hobbs, RN, BSN
Reflections on Nursing Leadership

DECEMBER 4

Responses to suffering include being willing to speak out against the travesties against the human spirit. It is leading the community response to violence, discrimination, homelessness, teen pregnancy, hunger, and the loneliness of aging.

—Judy Sadler, RN, PhD
Reflections on Nursing Leadership

DECEMBER 5

According to Loretta [Ford], every day should be devoted to improving oneself in every way possible. Her creed of "be in a hurry, there is not a moment to waste" is a leadership cry she applies first to herself and then to those around her.

—Beth Houser, RN, DNSc, FNP-C, CNAA, and Kathy Player, RN, EdD
Pivotal Moments in Nursing, Volume I

DECEMBER 6

Interest in being a mentor also includes understanding the needs and desires of the protégé. It means knowing the protégé's strengths and limitations, learning style, and the way s/he approaches and relates to others.

—Fay L. Bower, DNSc, FAAN
Building and Managing a Career in Nursing

DECEMBER 7

We must create a culture of mentoring wherever we work; develop an everyday
mentoring mentality with each other; give voice to mentoring through our
research and anecdotal reports; and create innovative mentoring strategies for
leadership development.

—Connie Vance, RN, EdD, FAAN
Reflections on Nursing Leadership

DECEMBER 8

Life is logical. You structure and plan it, but it is also serendipitous. These
moments are available to everyone.

—Susan Sherman, MPH, PhD
Conversations With Leaders

DECEMBER 9

My view of one's life and the influences on it is that it's like research: you have
constants and you have variables. You can't change your genes and several other
constants, but you certainly can choose to make the most of the variables.

—Sue Hegyvary, RN, PhD, FAAN
Reflections on Nursing Leadership

DECEMBER 10

The first five years of working as a nurse may center solely on patient care. After this, the pendulum starts to swing, as one progresses in his or her career. In addition to caring for patients, there is a sense of wanting to give back to the profession in an expanded role. Whether one takes on the role of preceptor, mentor, educator, researcher, or manager, the journey into leadership begins.

—Beth Houser, RN, DNSc, FNP-C, CNAA, and Kathy Player, RN, EdD
Reflections on Nursing Leadership

DECEMBER 11

The purpose [of mentoring] is twofold. First, it enables inexperienced nurses to become skilled in difficult psychomotor concepts. Second, mentoring allows new nurses to grow professionally while developing leadership skills.

—Theresa A. Granger, MN, ARNP, NP-C
Reflections on Nursing Leadership

DECEMBER 12

Mentors are not preceptors. Preceptors assist nurses technically, while mentors assist nurses by helping to shape character and professional competence.

—Theresa A. Granger, MN, ARNP, NP-C
Reflections on Nursing Leadership

DECEMBER 13

It's easy to get comfortable in a job and not be continuously career-minded and adventurous. Relatively few women are in top healthcare roles. To get to the top of any organization entails some degree of risk. I think women and certainly nurses in the future who aspire to such positions will break some of those glass ceilings.

—Nancy M. Valentine, RN, PhD, MPH, FAAN
Reflections on Nursing Leadership

DECEMBER 14

To be a positive mentor, I believe it is important to nurture, reinforce, encourage, and practice those skills and characteristics of leadership and to instill that ability in the person being mentored.

—Billye Brown, RN, EdD, FAAN
Reflections on Nursing Leadership

DECEMBER 15

Imagine the amplified effect of an established nurse who, though willing to fill a leadership position, opts instead to encourage a new member to take on the responsibility and then energetically assists that person in fulfilling that role. Such inclusiveness is a must if the generations are to make the most of what each has to offer.

—Jennifer L. Hobbs, RN, BSN
Reflections on Nursing Leadership

DECEMBER 16

Leaders must repeatedly mobilize others around new ideas, new information, and new experiences to create value, grow their niche, and sustain advantage. To do this, leaders must learn to build organizational capacity to adapt, whether they lead a large company or small community group.

—Nancy Dickenson-Hazard, RN, MSN, FAAN
Reflections on Nursing Leadership

DECEMBER 17

Professional or personal leadership success is based on hard work, commitment, and passion. Making it look effortless is the hallmark of a leader.

—Beth Houser, RN, DNSc, FNP-C, CNAA, and Kathy Player, RN, EdD
Pivotal Moments in Nursing, Volume I

DECEMBER 18

Nurses complain about all that is wrong with the nursing profession or healthcare, but we are not going to change anything if we don't break out and influence the agenda from the outside.

—Judith Shamian, RN, PhD, CHE
Pivotal Moments in Nursing, Volume II

DECEMBER 19

Opportunities to apply mentoring strategies to the worldwide nursing community increase as people of the world become more connected and the nursing profession becomes more globally focused.

—Mary W. Byrne, MPH, PhD, CPNP, and Maureen R. Keefe, RN, PhD, FAAN
Journal of Nursing Scholarship

DECEMBER 20

Empowerment begins with having a strong sense of what you can do and not letting others define your work as merely derivative—either handmaiden or being a physician substitute.

—Angela Barron McBride, RN, PhD, FAAN
Conversations With Leaders

DECEMBER 21

For the sake of their patients and for their own job fulfillment, nurses need a supportive work environment. Instead of eating our young, we need to focus our energies on supporting and nurturing one another.

—Theresa A. Granger, MN, ARNP, NP-C
Reflections on Nursing Leadership

DECEMBER 22

Leaders recognize early that no man is an island and quickly garner, foster, and build collaborative teams. They make it possible for people to do good work by trusting and enabling them.

—Nancy Dickenson-Hazard, RN, MSN, FAAN
Reflections on Nursing Leadership

DECEMBER 23

[Nurses] have to take on political and policy roles at all levels of government and governance. Make sure you do not experience "nursing amnesia." When you do take on leadership roles outside of nursing—do not forget that you are a nurse.

—Judith Shamian, RN, PhD, CHE
Reflections on Nursing Leadership

DECEMBER 24

The accomplishments of any president are the accomplishments of a smart team of hard-working, creative, and courageous people.

—Billye Brown, RN, EdD, FAAN
Reflecting on 30 Years of Nursing Leadership: 1975-2005

DECEMBER 25

Great leaders have the wisdom to know when to subordinate to the more competent team member. More importantly, the leader recognizes that by doing so, his choice increases rather than marginalizes his leadership credibility.

—Richard Carmona, RN, MD, MPH, FACS
Pivotal Moments in Nursing, Volume II

DECEMBER 26

In every age a few great souls are sent to dwell among us. The radiance of Virginia Henderson's light allowed many to bask directly and indirectly in its rays, as she steadfastly went about her soul's business. She observed the near with profound insight; she measured the far with care and wisdom. Her path allowed others to follow where none had traveled before.

—Eleanor Krohn Herrmann, RN, EdD, FAAN
Virginia Avenel Henderson: Signature for Nursing

DECEMBER 27

The fact that the most prolific educators form emotionally supportive and intellectually challenging partnerships suggests a link between collaborative relationships and knowledge advancement. In consulting with nursing faculty groups, I find that the more collaboration is valued, the fewer the joy-stealing games and the greater the productivity of teachers and scholars.

—Kathleen T. Heinrich, RN, PhD
Reflections on Nursing Leadership

DECEMBER 28

Be aware that to everything there is a season, with unforeseen storms and sunshine in between. Know that regardless of where you find yourself, eventually you will have to leave the mountain top. When that time comes, leave not with bitterness or despair, but leave with the joy of having had the opportunity to experience the view from the top.

—Barbara Nichols, RN, DHL, MS, FAAN
Conversations With Leaders

DECEMBER 29

Insanity is doing the same things over and over again and expecting different results.

—Unknown

DECEMBER 30

Reach for the stars knowing that, one day, you will capture the light, warmth, and brilliance that only leadership experience can offer.

—Beth Houser, RN, DNSc, FNP-C, CNAA, and Kathy Player, RN, EdD
Reflections on Nursing Leadership

Nursing is going to save the future of healthcare!

—Florence Schorske Wald, RN, MN, MS, FAAN
Pivotal Moments in Nursing, Volume II

Notes

Bibliography

Bower, F.L. (2000). *Nurses taking the lead*: *Personal qualities of effective leadership*. Philadelphia: W.B. Saunders.

Contemporary issues in nursing, volume II. (2006). Indianapolis, IN: Sigma Theta Tau International.

Donley, R. (2005). *Reflecting on 30 years of nursing leadership: 1975-2005*. Indianapolis, IN: Sigma Theta Tau International.

Dreher, M. (n.d.). *Quote....end quote*. Online at http://www.uiowa.edu/~fyi/issues/issues2006_v43/06052006/quote.html

Dreher, M., Shapiro, D., & Asselin, M. (2006). *Healthy places, healthy people: A handbook for culturally competent community nursing practice*. Indianapolis, IN: Sigma Theta Tau International.

Hanson-Turton, T., Sherman, S., & Ferguson, V.D. (Eds.). (2007). *Conversations with leaders: Lessons from the frontlines*. Indianapolis, IN: Sigma Theta Tau International.

Hermann, E.K. (1998). *Virginia Avenel Henderson: Signature for nursing*. Indianapolis, IN: Sigma Theta Tau International.

Houser, B., & Player, K. (2004). *Pivotal moments in nursing, volume 1*. Indianapolis, IN: Sigma Theta Tau International.

Houser, B., & Player, K. (2007). *Pivotal moments in nursing, volume II*. Indianapolis, IN: Sigma Theta Tau International.

Journal of Nursing Scholarship. Indianapolis, IN: Sigma Theta Tau International.

Kouzes, J., & Posner, B. (2002). The leadership challenge. San Francisco: Jossey Bass.

Marquis, B.L., & Huston, C.J. (2003). *Leadership roles and management functions in nursing: Theory & application* (4th ed.). Philadelphia: Lippincott.

Miller, T.W. (Ed.). (2003). *Building and managing a career in nursing: Strategies for advancing your career.* Indianapolis, IN: Sigma Theta Tau International.

Porter-O'Grady, T., & Malloch, K. (2003). *Quantum leadership: A textbook of new leadership.* Sudbury, MA: Jones & Bartlett.

Reflections on Nursing Leadership (formerly known as *Reflections).* Indianapolis, IN: Sigma Theta Tau International.

Sullivan, E. (Ed.). (1999). *Creating nursing's future: Issues, opportunities and challenges.* St. Louis, MO: Mosby.

Sullivan, E. (n.d.). *The rules of the game.* Online at http://www.eleanorsullivan.com/pdf/The_Rules_of_the_Game.pdf

Sullivan, E. (n.d.). *Taking the mystery out of influence.* Online at http://www.eleanorsullivan.com/pdf/Taking_the_Mystery_Out_of_Influence.pdf

Wendler, C. (Ed.). (2005). *The heART of nursing* (2nd ed.). Indianapolis, IN: Sigma Theta Tau International.

Zemke, R., Raines, C., & Filipczak, B. (2000). *Generations at work.* New York: AMACOM Publishing.

Index of Authors

Adams-Ender, Clara, RN, MSN, CNAA, FAAN, 5, 29, 64

Aiken, Linda, RN, PhD, FAAN, FRCN, 7

Ang, Roselin, RN, MSN; and Fong, Long Chooi, RN, MSc, 44, 74

Anonymous, 85

Barton, Clara, 32

Beese-Bjurstrom, Shawna, RN, BSN, C, CCRN, 153

Boman, Jeanette, RN, PhD, 108

Bostick, Cynthia, RN, CS, PhD, 12

Bower, Fay L., DNSc, FAAN, 6, 31, 51, 63, 72, 76, 104, 128, 135, 141, 144, 154

Brown, Billye, RN, EdD, FAAN, 29, 46, 103, 157, 160

Brown, Sharon A., RN, MSN, 17

Butterworth, Tony, CBE, PhD, RMN, RGN, FRCN, FmedSci, FRCPsych, 18, 89

Byrne, Mary W., MPH, PhD, CPNP; and Keefe, Maureen R., RN, PhD, FAAN, 130, 159

Cangelosi, Pamela R., RNC, PhD, 22, 78, 99

Carmona, Richard, RN, MD, MPH, FACS, 5, 24, 56, 66, 106, 107, 153, 161

Carroll, Theresa L., RN, PhD; and Austin, Tommye, RN, MSN, 78, 148

Carter, Rosalynn, 120

Chater, Shirley Sears, RN, PhD, FAAN, 3, 49

Chen, Hsiu-Chin, RN, PhD, EdD; Beck, Susan L., PhD, APRN, FAAN; and Amos, Linda K., RN, EdD, FAAN, 76

Clarke-Tasker, Veronica, RN, PhD, MBA, 91

Clifford, Joyce, RN, PhD, FAAN, 8, 86

Conway-Welch, Colleen, RN, PhD, FAAN, 142

Curtin, Leah, RN, DSc, MS, MA, FAAN, 25, 114

D'Anna, Barbara Ann, RN, MSN, CNOR, 143

Daniels, Melodie, RN, 21

de Tornyay, Rheba, RN, EdD, FAAN, 37

Dickenson-Hazard, Nancy, RN, MNS, FAAN, 6, 7, 10, 11, 21, 30, 34, 37, 38, 43, 45, 48, 57, 52, 73, 79, 84, 85, 87, 100, 103, 104, 106, 107, 128, 144, 148, 149, 158, 160

Dreher, Melanie C., RN, PhD, FAAN, 23, 61, 87, 107, 120

Dreher, Melanie C., RN, PhD, FAAN; Shapiro, Dolores J., RN, PhD; and Asselin, Micheline, RN, MPA, MSN, CHPN, 46

Dumas, Rhetaugh Graves, RN, PhD, FAAN, 104

Eisner, Jane, 131

Elders, Jocelyn, MD, 84

Fagin, Claire, RN, PhD, FAAN, 32, 121

Ferguson, Vernice, RN, MA, FAAN, FRCN, 29, 101, 129, 131

Fitzpatrick, Joyce, RN, MBA, PhD, FAAN, 30

Ford, Loretta, RN, EdD, PNP, FAAN, FAANP, 112

Freshwater, Dawn, RGN, PhD, BA, RNT, FRCN, 32, 56, 70, 87, 134, 141

Fullam, Charlene, RN, MA, CEN, 92, 112, 133

Fulmer, Terry, RN, PhD, FAAN, 142

Graham, Iain, RN, MEd, MSc, PhD, 9, 16, 94, 101, 113, 143

Granger, Theresa A., MN, ARNP, NP-C, 35, 125, 139, 156, 159

Gray, Genevieve, RN, MSc, Dip Adv Nurs Studs, Dip Ned, CM, FRCNA, FCN (NSW), 21, 134

Hansen-Turton, Tine, MGA, 142

Hassmiller, Susan B., RN, PhD, FAAN, 47, 51, 63, 91, 98, 101, 118

Hatýpoðlu, F. Sevgi, RN, PhD, 39

Hegyvary, Sue, RN, PhD, FAAN, 155

Heinrich, Kathleen T., RN, PhD, 161

Herrmann, Eleanor Krohn, RN, EdD, FAAN, 161

Hinshaw, Ada Sue, RN, PhD, FAAN, 16

Hisama, Kay Keiko, RN, PhD, 133

Hobbs, Jennifer L., RN, BSN, 20, 60, 106, 117, 125, 153, 157

Houser, Beth, RN, DNSc, FNP-C, CNAA; and Player, Kathy, RN, EdD, 2, 19, 20, 57, 58, 60, 64, 65, 73, 74, 77, 84, 89, 90, 98, 99, 102, 112, 113, 116, 118, 128, 131, 132, 134, 140, 144, 145, 147, 154, 156, 158, 162

International Leadership Institute, Honor Society of Nursing, Sigma Theta Tau International, 4, 8, 11, 16, 20, 23, 100, 129

Jerzack, Linda, RN, NP, 22

Johns, Christopher, PhD, 113

Kauss, Judith B., RN, MSN, FAAN, 132

Kelly, Lucie S., RN, PhD, FAAN, 59

Kerfoot, Karlene M., RN, PhD, CAAN, FAAN; and Steven S. Ivy, MDiv, PhD, 10

Kinsey, Katherine, RN, PhD, FAAN, 85

Klein, Eric, BA, 5, 76, 93

Klein, Eric, BA; and Dickenson-Hazard, Nancy, RN, MSN, FAAN, 18, 25, 47, 57, 61, 75, 80, 86, 88, 102, 117, 118, 135

Koloroutis, Mary, RN, MS; and Felgen, Jayne, RN, MPA, 91, 148

Lee, Carla A. Bouska, PhD, ARNP, C, CNS, 36

Lubic, Ruth, CNM, EdD, FAAN, FACNM, 70, 125

Lyon, Brenda L. RN, DNS, FAAN, 114, 116

Marquis, Bessie L., RN, CNAA, MSN; and Huston, Carol J., RN, CNAA, MSN, DPA, 7, 50, 71, 116

McBride, Angela Barron, RN, PhD, FAAN, 8, 121, 146, 159

McClure, Margaret, RN, PhD, FAAN, 36, 46, 127, 149

Meleis, Afaf, RN, PhD, FAAN, 126

Melnyk, Bernadette Mazurek, RN, PhD, CPNP, NPP, FAAN, FNAP; and Fineout- Overholt, Ellen, RN, PhD, 11, 114

Milazzo, Vickie L., RN, MSN, JD, 43

Mother Theresa, 4, 24, 90

Nichols, Barbara, RN, DHL, MS, FAAN, 129, 146, 162

Nightingale, Florence, 48, 59, 119

Parfitt, Barbara A., RGN, RM, FNP, PhD, 119

Pearson, Alan, RN, ONC, DipNEd, DANS, MSc, PhD, FCN(NSW), FINA, FRCNA, FAAG, FRCN, 33, 93

Peña, Laura Morán, RN, EdM, 58, 65

Pesut, Daniel J., APRN, BC, PhD, FAAN, 35, 60, 88, 103

Picard, Carol A., RN, PhD, 86, 98

Porter-O'Grady, Tim, RN, PhD, FAAN, 38, 79

Porter-O'Grady, Tim, RN, PhD, FAAN; and Malloch, Kathy, RN, MBA, PhD, FAAN, 31, 50, 65, 147

Post-White, Janice, RN, PhD, FAAN, 50, 115

Sadler, Judy, RN, PhD, 19, 154

Salmon, Marla E., RN, ScD, FAAN, 2, 51, 70, 127, 139, 143

Saunders, Dame Cicely, OM, DBE, 58

Shamian, Judith, RN, PhD, CHE, 63, 158, 160

Sherman, Susan, MPH, PhD, 155

Shirey, Maria R., RN, MS, MBA, FACHE, CNAA, BC, 3, 18, 34, 48, 49, 56, 71, 75, 117, 126, 139

Sieg, Diane, RN, CLC, 80

Sills, Grayce, RN, PhD, 17, 45, 52, 59

Smith, Gloria, RN, PhD, FAAN, 33, 77, 126, 147

Spear, Hila J., RN, PhD, 44

Stainton, M. Colleen, RN, DNSc, FCN(NSW), 72

Stevens, Kathleen R., RN, EdD, FAAN, 62

Stuenkel, Diane L., RN, MS, 6, 61, 90, 115

Styles, Gretta, RN, EdD, FAAN, 22, 37, 47

Sullivan, Eleanor, RN, PhD, FAAN, 4, 34, 62, 93, 127, 141

Tagliareni, Salvatore, PhD, 130

Tamez, Eloisa G., RN, PhD, FAAN, 3

Thompson, Patricia E., RN, EdD, 10, 44, 92, 100, 115

Titler, Marita G., RN, PhD, FAAN; Cullen, Laura, RN, MA; and Ardery, Gail, RN, PhD, 9, 88

Trent, Barbara A., RN, EdD, 105, 120, 133

Unknown, 140, 162

Valentine, Nancy M., RN, PhD, MPH, FAAN, 157

Vance, Connie, RN, EdD, FAAN, 36, 121, 155

Vance, Connie, RN, EdD, FAAN; and Larson, Elaine, RN, PhD, FAAN, 62, 130

Wakefield, Mary, RN, PhD, 2, 24, 72, 89, 102, 145

Wald, Florence Schorske, RN, MN, MS, FAAN, 23, 43, 73, 105, 163

Watson, Jean, RN, PhD, HNC, FAAN, 140

Wieck, K. Lynn, RN, PhD; Prydun, Margaret, RN, PhD; and Walsh, Terri, RN, MS, 45, 71, 77, 92

Woody, Mary, RN, MA, FAAN, 119